AF349965

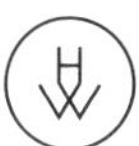

In the Studio, a new series from Hauser & Wirth Publishers, gives readers a behind-the-scenes view of artists at work. Each book focuses on a major figure of twentieth- or twenty-first-century art, offering an introduction to their influences, materials, and techniques. Written by leading scholars and critics and generously illustrated, *In the Studio* titles are the perfect companion for longstanding art lovers and newcomers alike.

The first volumes in the series explore the life and work of Phyllida Barlow and Jack Whitten; forthcoming books focus on Berlinde De Bruyckere, Louise Bourgeois, and Paul McCarthy.

Lucrezia Calabrò Visconti is a writer and the head curator at the Istituto Svizzero in Rome, Milan, and Palermo. She was previously the chief curator at the Pinacoteca Agnelli, Turin, where she co-curated the retrospective exhibition *Lee Lozano: Strike* and edited the accompanying publication. Her exhibitions include monographic surveys of Pauline Boudry and Renate Lorenz (2025), Salvo (2024), and Sylvie Fleury (2022), and she has curated new commissions by Dominique Gonzales-Foerster (2023), Lucy McKenzie (2023), and Mark Leckey (2022), among others. In 2018 she curated the Moscow International Biennale for Young Art. She is the co-founder and vice president of Art Workers Italia.

Lucrezia
Calabrò
Visconti

Lee
Lozano

Hauser & Wirth Publishers

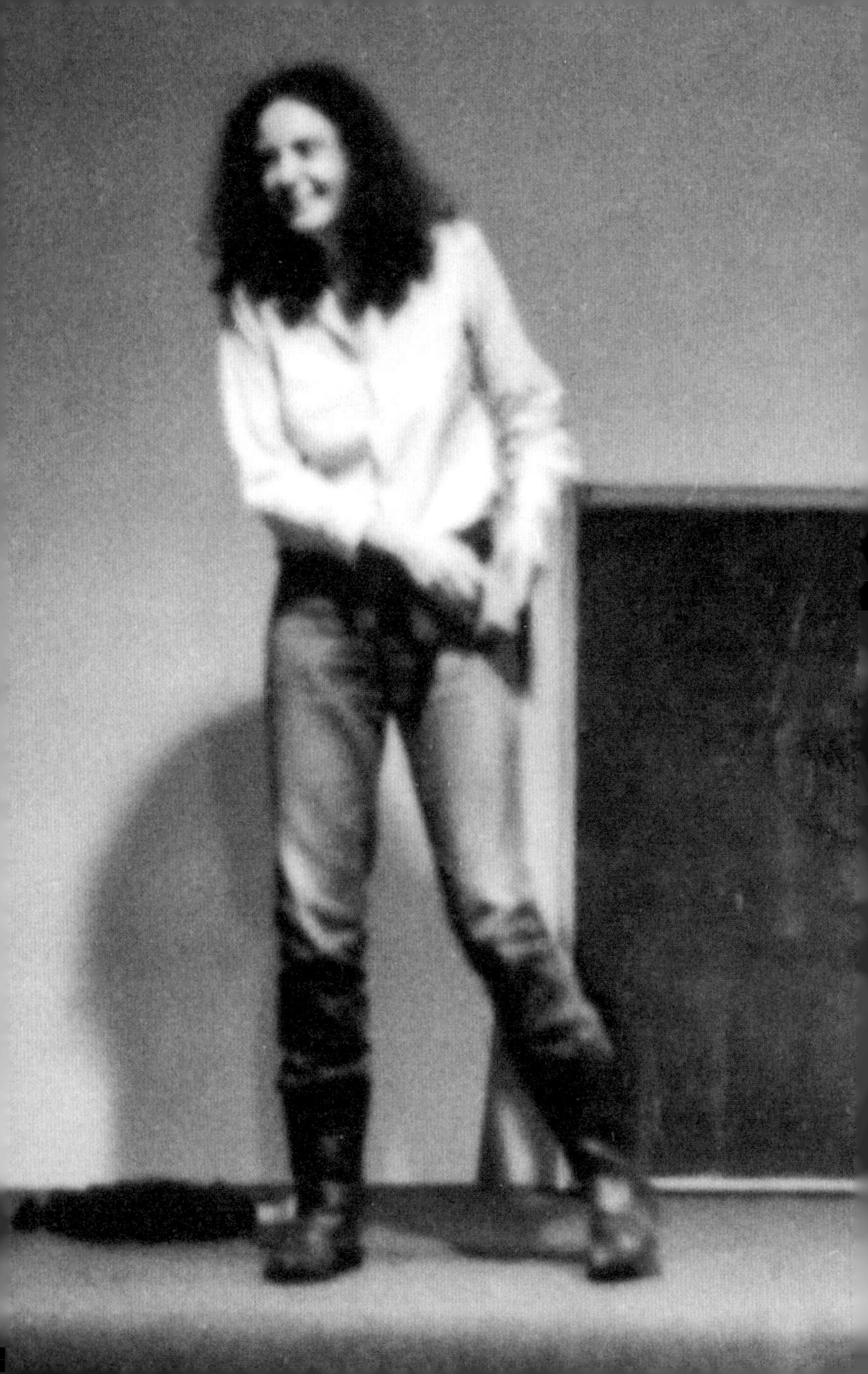

"Ideas are the most powerful thing in the world."

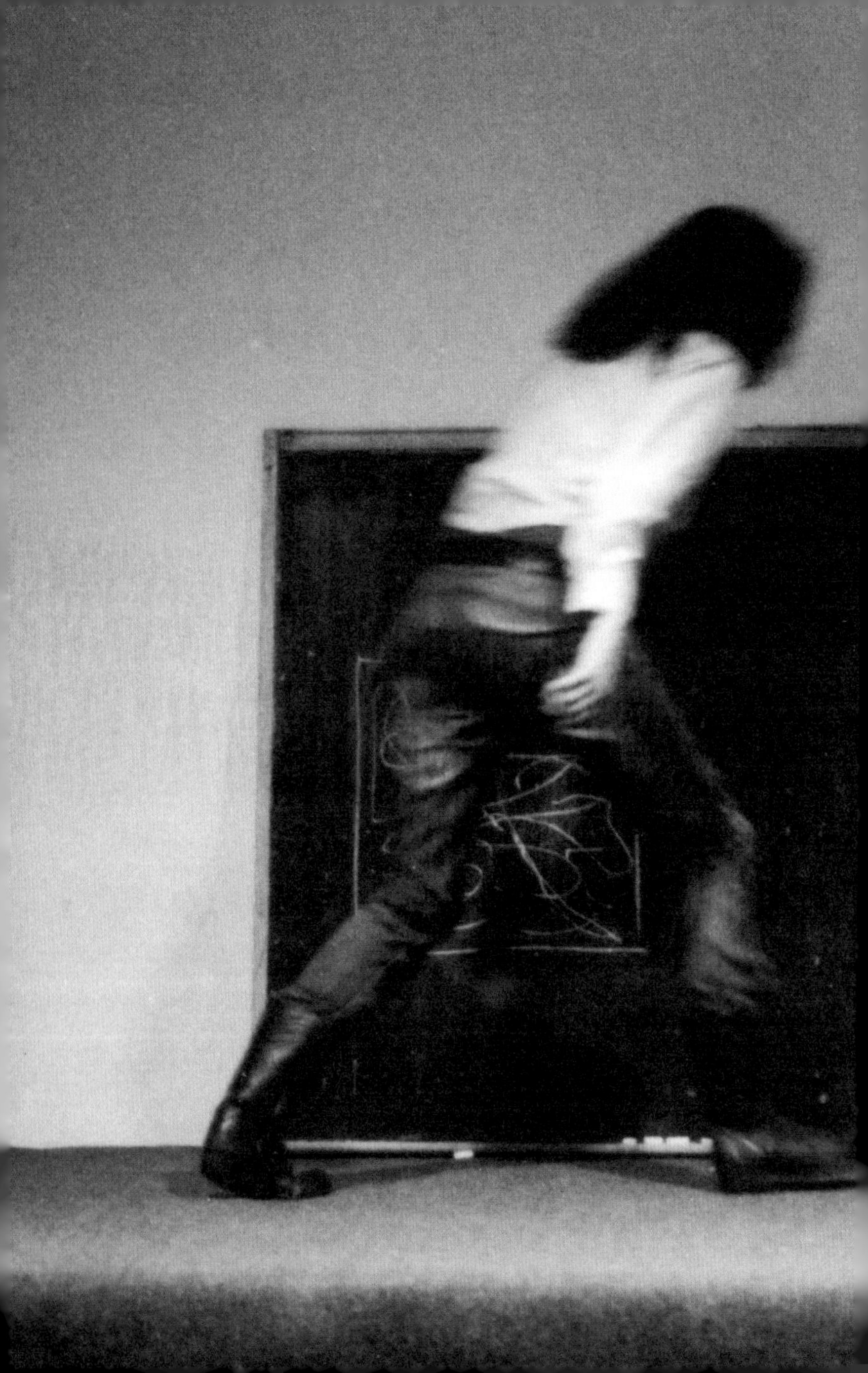

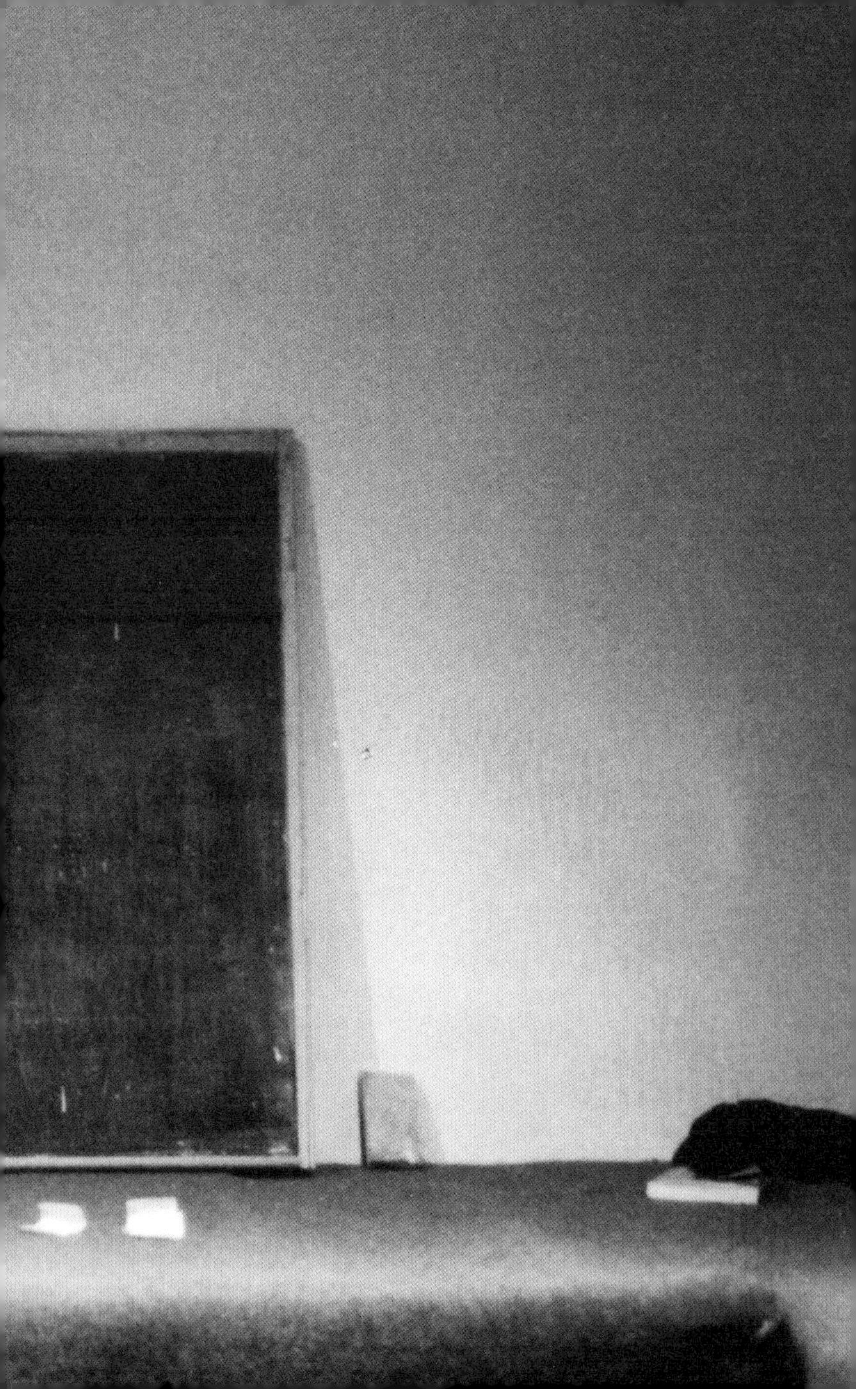

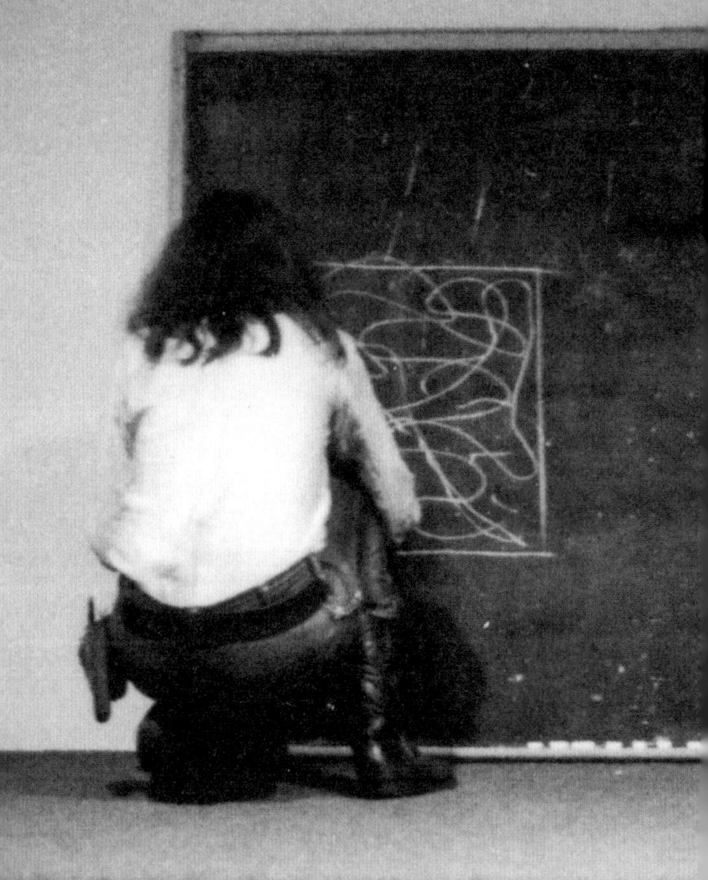

"Making art is the
greatest act of all."

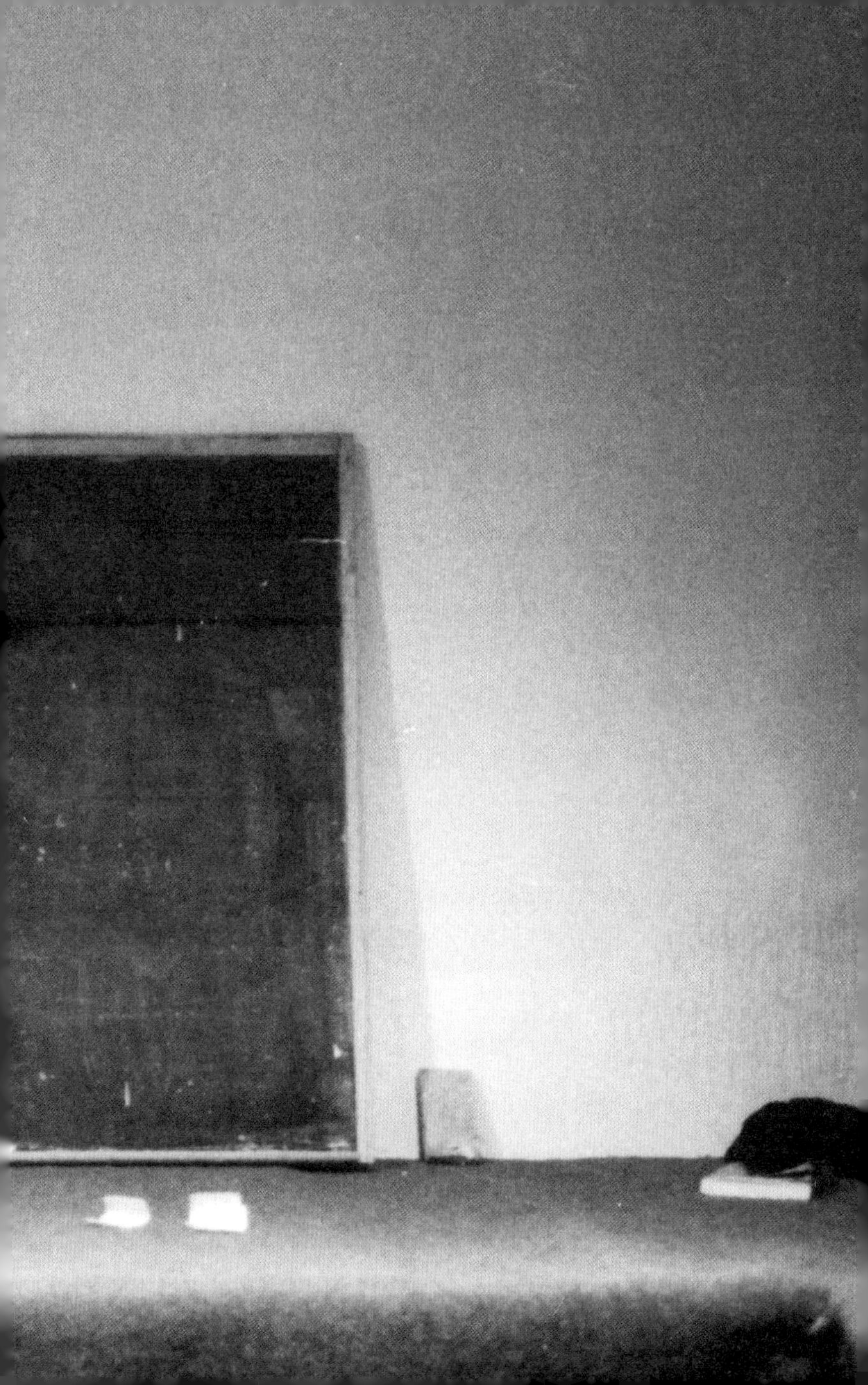

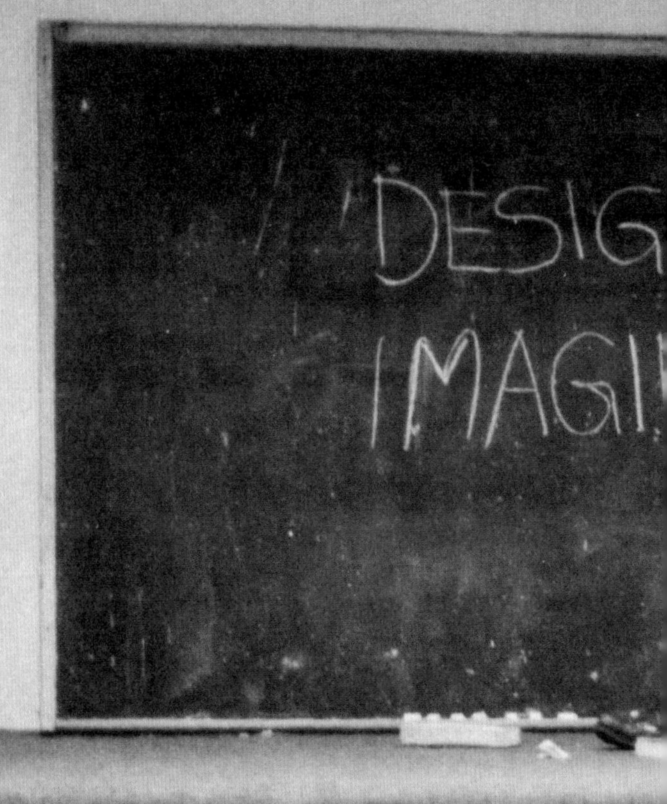
DESIG
IMAGI

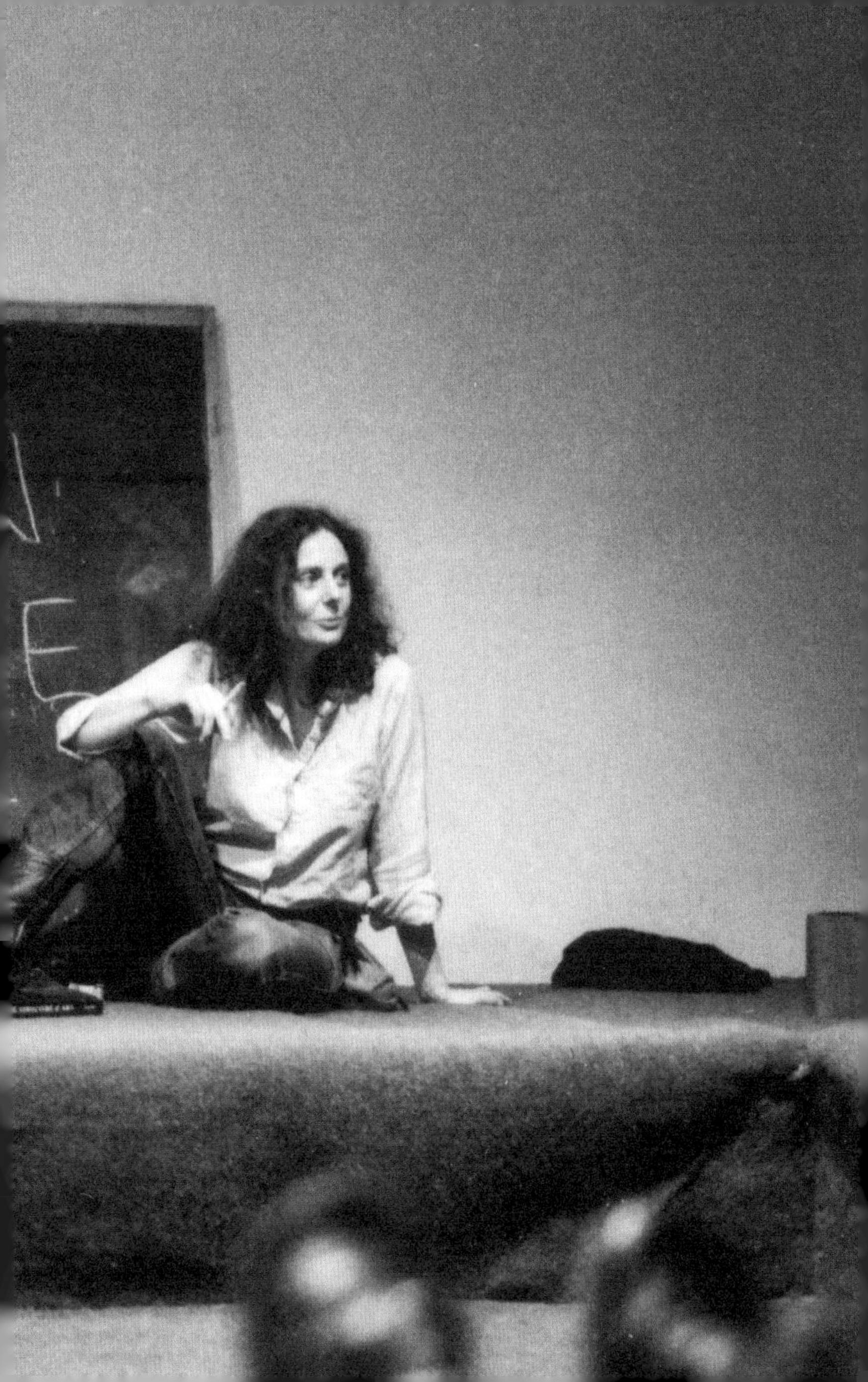

Contents

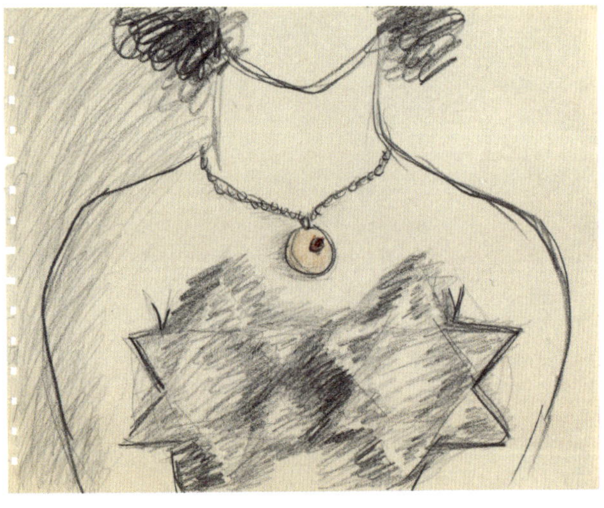

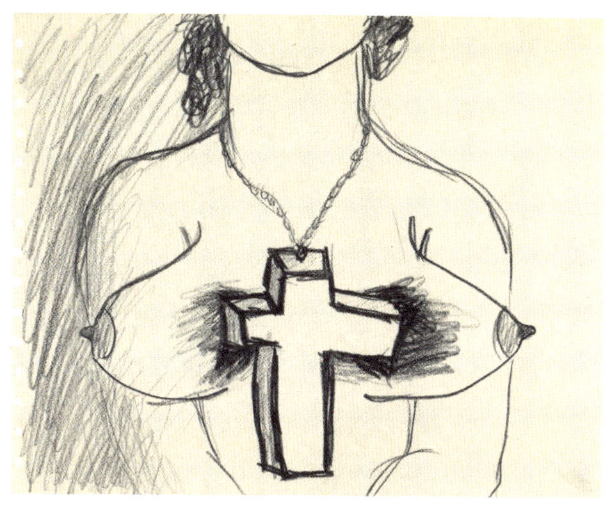

FEB 22, 69

DICK:

☰☷   HAS TURNED INTO ☵☷.

I APOLOGISE FOR MY BAD BEHAVIOR
BUT IT HAD TO BE. GOING THROUGH
VIOLENT CHANGES.

DON'T BELIEVE ANYTHING YOU HEAR
ABOUT ME.

LOVE, LEE

No title, 1969. Ink on paper, 11 × 8½ in. (28 × 21.5 cm)

"Don't believe anything
you hear about me"

On February 22, 1969, in a note addressed to her friend
and gallerist Richard Bellamy, Lee Lozano solemnly
declared: "Dick…I apologise for my bad behavior but
it had to be. Going through violent changes. Don't believe
anything you hear about me." Adding to the gravity of
the message, hovering above it was a result from the *I Ching*
(or *Book of Changes*), the Chinese oracle that accompanied
many of the artist's decisions at the time: "䷖ has turned
into ䷗." "Stripping" has turned into "Returning."

Two weeks earlier, on February 8, Lozano had decided
to pull her painting from a three-person show that was
about to open at Noah Goldowsky Gallery, where Bellamy
was director. Regarding this choice, she wrote in her
notebooks: "I can't 'hang' with work that brings me down."
We don't know whether it was then or later on, after more
cautious consideration, that Lozano framed her action
as *Withdrawal Piece*.

Withdrawal Piece would be just one of a long series of
renunciations—often coinciding with deliberate acts of
self-sabotage—that marked the next two years of Lozano's
life. In many cases, these actions were experiments she
referred to as "Life-Art" pieces (pp. 29–39): gestures,
actions, and experiences elevated to conceptual artworks
through the strategic addition of a single, yet potent, word—
piece. A few months later came *General Strike Piece* (p. 33):
her gradual withdrawal from uptown art-world functions
and gatherings, in order to dedicate herself exclusively to
the pursuit of "total personal & public revolution." About a

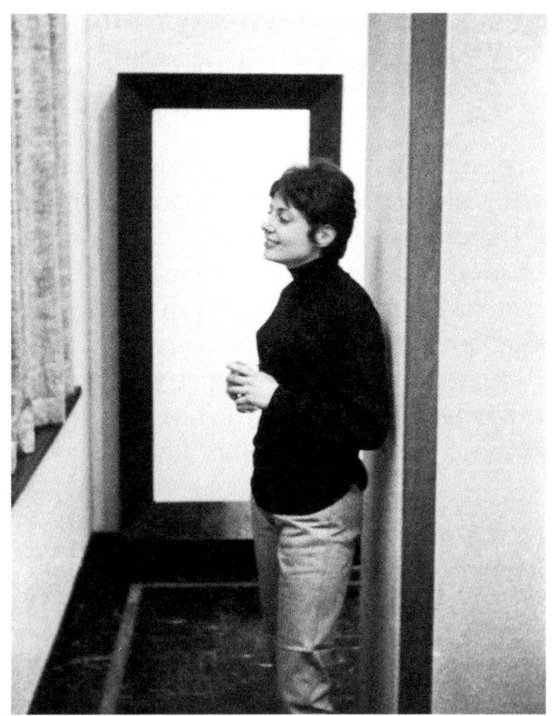

Lozano at the opening of *The New Art*, Davison Center, Wesleyan University, Middletown, Connecticut, 1964

year later she formalized the even more radical *Dropout Piece* (p. 107)—according to Lozano herself, "the <u>hardest work</u> I have ever done." Even if the outcomes of her "dropout" are largely shrouded in mystery, after 1972 Lozano lost interest in exhibiting work, severed nearly all her active social relationships, and, after a hiatus spent flying under the radar in the city, relocated to Texas, where she lived until her death in 1999. The decision to quit Bellamy's exhibition in 1969 was an initial challenge to herself, a test to see just how bad her behavior could get before it began to seriously damage her relationships.

Life and Work

Flashback to ten years earlier: it was Bellamy who had
introduced Lozano to the New York scene. Lozano was
living in Chicago, where she had moved in 1948 from her
native Newark, New Jersey, to study science and philosophy.
She later enrolled in painting at the city's Art Institute,
determined to become an artist. By 1960 she had landed
in New York—a decision premeditated as early as 1955.
There, she connected with Bellamy, who was then running
the Green Gallery, one of the most prominent avant-garde
spaces in the city. Around it, a new generation of artists was
gathering, diverse in their practices yet united by a shared
decision to turn their backs on Abstract Expressionism.

Lozano joined that scene early on, and spent the
following twelve years rapping, hanging out, getting
high, occasionally hooking up, and, crucially, sparring
and sharing ideas with some key figures of contemporary
art at the time. According to her meticulously kept
notebooks, these included Carl Andre, Hollis Frampton,
Dan Graham, Stephen Kaltenbach, Sol LeWitt, Lucy
Lippard, Robert Morris, and many others who could be
found lingering between the openings of uptown galleries,
the hardware stores on Canal Street, and the barstools
of Max's Kansas City.

Minimalism (in sculpture, painting, and music), Pop art,
and Conceptualism dominated the art scene. The rise
of Conceptual art, in particular, was partly a reaction to
the rampant commercialization of the art world and the
increasing commodification of the art object. The end of
the decade, especially, was marked by a response to—and,
progressively, reaction against—the structural issues of the
art system, shaped by inequalities and fueled by economic
powers complicit in social injustices and deadly enterprises

like the Vietnam War. This perspective aligned with a
decade known for the struggles of the civil rights movement,
the flourishing of so-called second-wave feminism, and
widespread protests against American imperialism and war.
Lozano found herself right at the center of these growing
energies in art and society, and often acted as a catalyst
for them. Despite this, her personal and total forms of
"cerebellion" fiercely rejected certain artistic mediums,
working methods, and political demands put forth by
her peers. Indeed, she was always determined to reprogram
such drives into an autonomous, obstinately solitary,
and at times overtly hostile path.

Although Lozano wrote to Bellamy, "don't believe anything
you hear about me," she, herself, was the one person he
should have been wary of trusting. Decoys, false clues,
sudden changes of course, and categorical statements
betrayed by obvious truths peppered Lozano's behavior
constantly—and, in large part, intentionally. "Seek the
extremes, that's where the action is," she claimed, and
therefore she wrote private notebooks only to ensure they
were found; she declared a general strike against art events,
then devised a *Dialogue Piece* (pp. 114–21) that forced
the very people she would have encountered at those
events to talk with her; she fantasized about becoming a
Zen master to guide women toward enlightenment, then
chose to stop speaking to them entirely for the rest of her
life; she reached the peak of her career and, at that same
moment, decided to drop out of it altogether.

Tracing Lozano's footsteps means embracing her
multidimensional, sometimes capricious, deliberately
enigmatic path, knowing that she might have concealed
her missteps with special effects, or left traps along the

way to buy herself some time to flee from us. Her multiple personas layer on top of each other, and it's up to us to dig through them in order to search for some clarity. As she wrote in one notebook: "Maybe the idea of 'destroy in order to create' is fallacious. Overlap or overlay works just as well most of the time and leaves something for the archaeologists to play around with." So here we are, devoted archaeologists, granted permission to look into the layers of "infofiction" she left behind for us to play with.

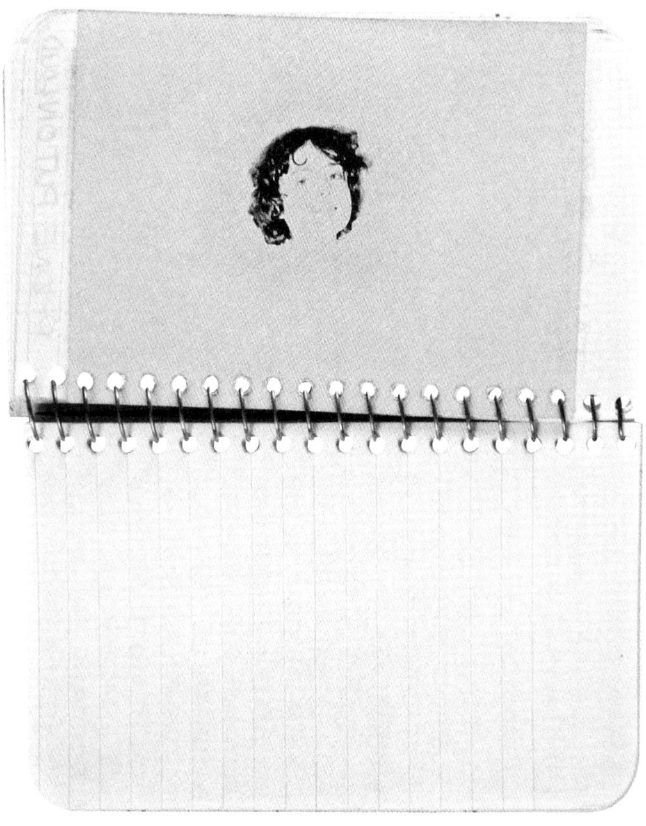

Lozano, photo from *Private Book 5*, December 31, 1969

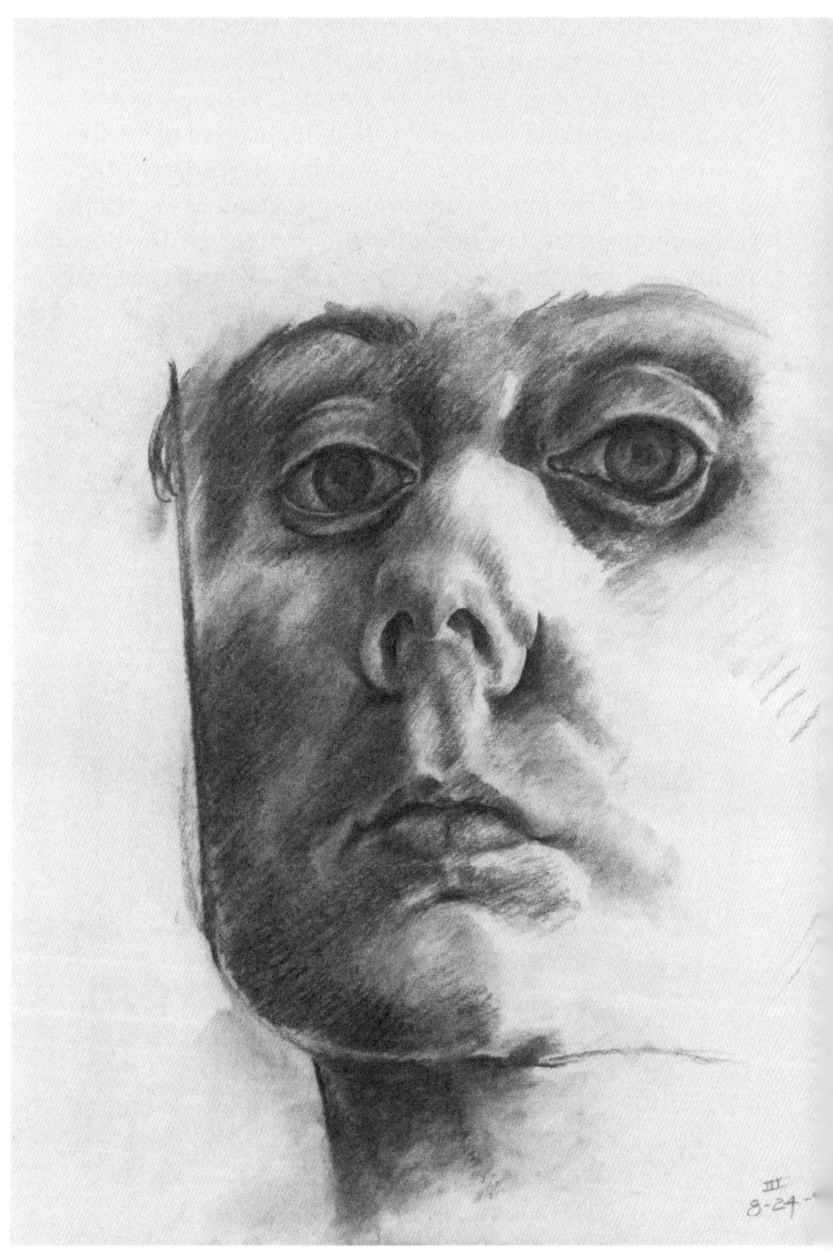

No title, 1959. Charcoal on paper, 25 × 18⅞ in. (63.5 × 48 cm)

"Everyone knows that an artist's best work often covers a very short period of time"

Lozano's artistic career is usually considered to last approximately twelve years, even if, since she declared her dropout as a legitimate artwork, it would be more accurate to say twelve years plus a single, twenty-seven-year-long, final work. In its briefer, pre-dropout phase, Lozano's artistic practice shifted—or, rather, switched ("the Scorpio version of shift")—from one series to the next, changing in subject, intention, scale, style, medium, and field. Yet, when looked at as a whole, each evolution seems like an inevitable outcome of the previous one. From her first drawings and paintings with expressionist undertones to the minimalist canvases that brought her success, from her conceptual experimentation to the subsequent, harder to pin down, final period of her work, it seems like Lozano's practice eventually grew too vast to be contained within the limits of art, leaving her no option but to break out of it.

In the early 1960s, her work centered on cartoonlike drawings and canvases that spewed vivid, pornographic, at times blasphemous imagery, where dissected bodies interacted with tools, household appliances, scrap materials, airplanes, and weapons. The items depicted seemed chosen mainly for the plausibility of their function to be perverted in compositions portraying erotic encounters, ferocious combat, or surrealistic, odd fusions between them and body parts—especially genitalia. Objects with a scandalous quality such as liturgical tools, or with comic potential such as stationery, cigars, and even a trumpet, were favored. Sometimes,

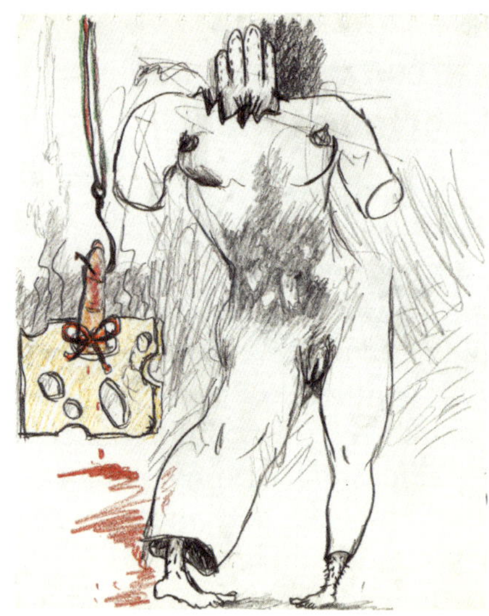

No title, 1960. Graphite and crayon on paper, 16¾ × 13⅞ in. (42.5 × 35.1 cm)

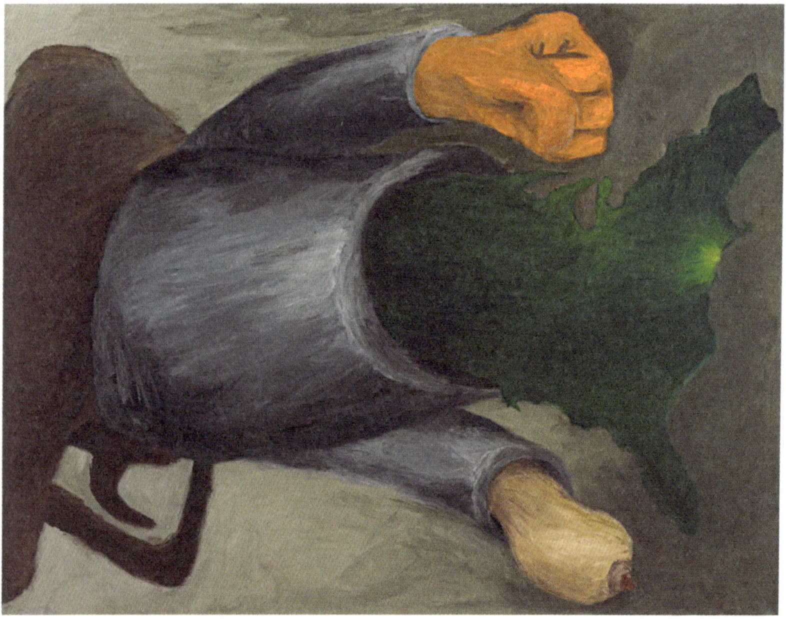

No title, 1963. Oil on canvas, 37¼ × 49⅝ in. (94.7 × 126 cm)

　　　　Life and Work

she introduced slogans reminiscent of early Pop art,
amplifying the visual indecency of the images with
a surplus of verbal profanity, often providing witty,
satirical commentary on contemporary society.

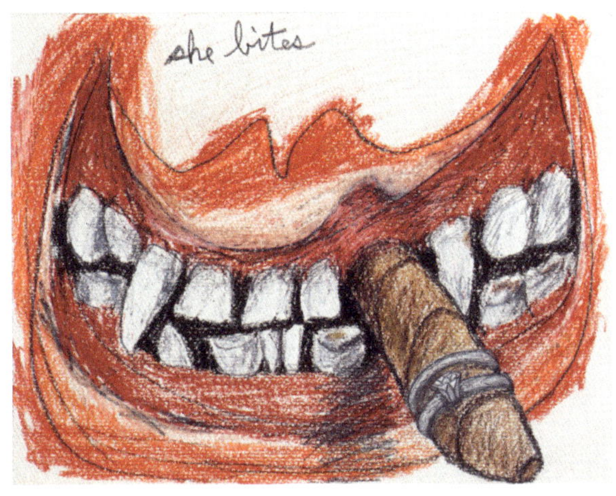

No title, 1963. Crayon on paper, 8¾ × 11¾ in. (22.2 × 30 cm)

Around 1963–64, the subject of work tools gradually took
center stage, occupying the entire surface of increasingly
large canvases. The energy of Lozano's early works—whether
electric, erotic, kinetic, or belligerent—translated into
monumental hammers, C-clamps, screws, bolts, and drill
bits, portrayed in dramatic tension. Forms were stretched,
enlarged, crammed into canvases that seemed too small
to contain them. Her painterly style grew less textural
and more concise, sharp, almost graphic. By 1965 she was
working on a series of new paintings, in which references
to real objects gave way to purely geometric forms (pp. 70–
79). These large canvases used a minimalist and abstract
vocabulary to evoke motion, charge, and force. The titles
referenced verbs: actions presumably performed by the

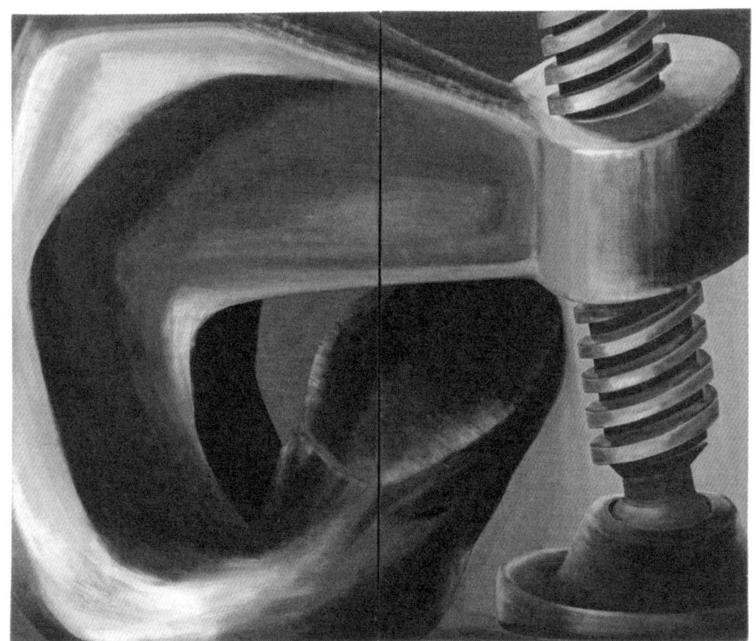

No title, 1964. Oil on canvas, two panels, 108⅜ × 132½ in. (275.2 × 336.5 cm)

tools from her previous series such as *spin*, *charge*, *switch*, *clamp*, and *breach*, but extended to a broader understanding of energy, increasingly influenced by Lozano's interest in hard sciences and spiritual disciplines.

The period from 1967 to 1970 saw Lozano engaged with three main streams of activity: the realization of the *Wave* series, the conception and evolution of her "Life-Art" pieces, and the gradual yet resolute decision to withdraw from the art scene. Despite their differences, these processes nurtured one another, finding fertile ground in her studio. The *Wave* series comprises eleven canvases, seven of them monochromatic, aimed at metaphorically representing the extended electromagnetic

        Life and Work

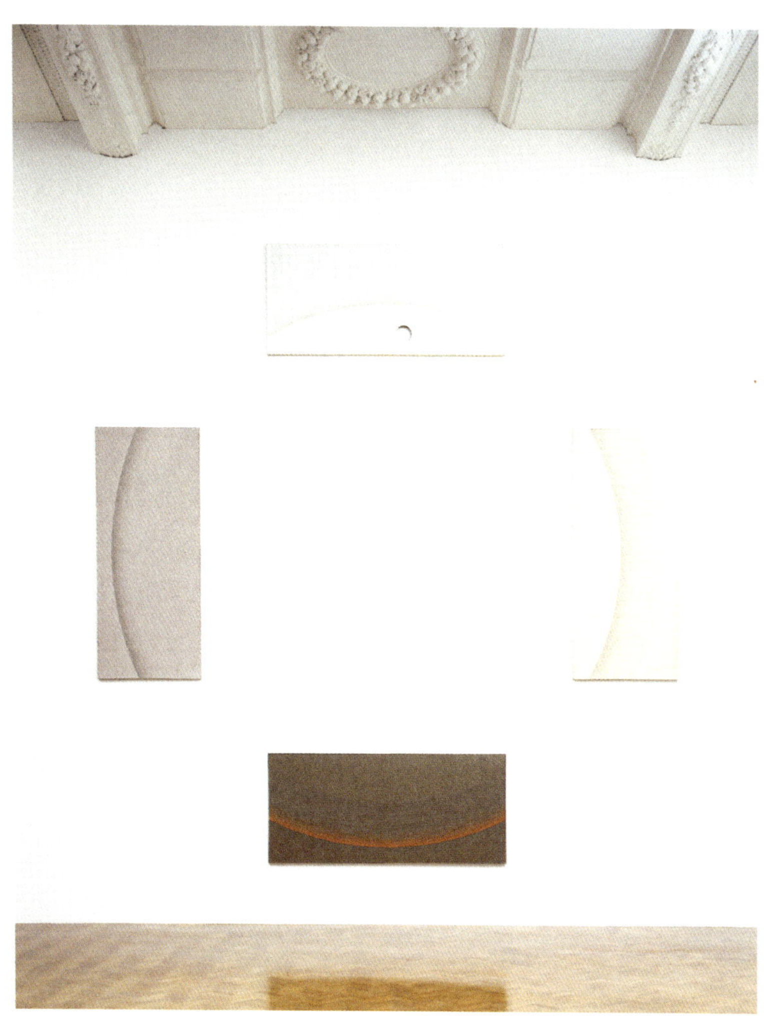

No title, 1969. Oil on canvas, four parts, 237 × 237 in. (602 × 602 cm) overall

METAPHOR

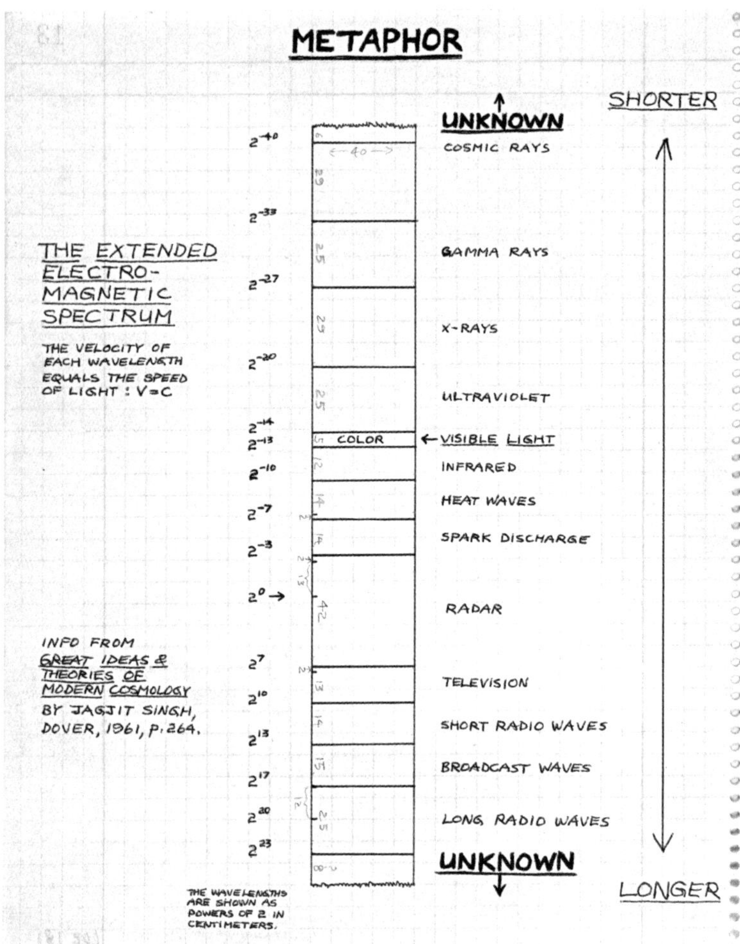

No title, n.d. Graphite and ink on paper, 11 × 8½ in. (28 × 21.5 cm)

spectrum (p. 26). Each canvas was produced in a single session, with Lozano recording data about her process (time taken, drugs consumed, energy levels, body coordination). Her painting practice overlapped with methods reminiscent of scientific experiments or durational performances, turning the canvas into one of the elements of a more complex system, a sort of material residue of her catalytic actions. She completed the paintings in 1970 for a solo show at the Whitney Museum of American Art (pp. 93–95), where the *Wave* series was exhibited alongside some of her conceptual works.

Lozano's conceptual practice, culminating in the so-called "Life-Art" pieces, started developing around 1968 alongside her painting activity. Her pieces were compiled in eleven "private notebooks," documenting the conceptual evolution of her work while chronicling her growing desire to expel herself from the art world. The notebooks contain about eighty "pieces" from 1969 to 1970, scattered among details of her daily, relational, and sexual life, as well as her emotional and mental states. These were partially contradicted, deepened, or censored through an overall edit done by Lozano in early 1972, before (supposedly) vanishing without leaving further traces.

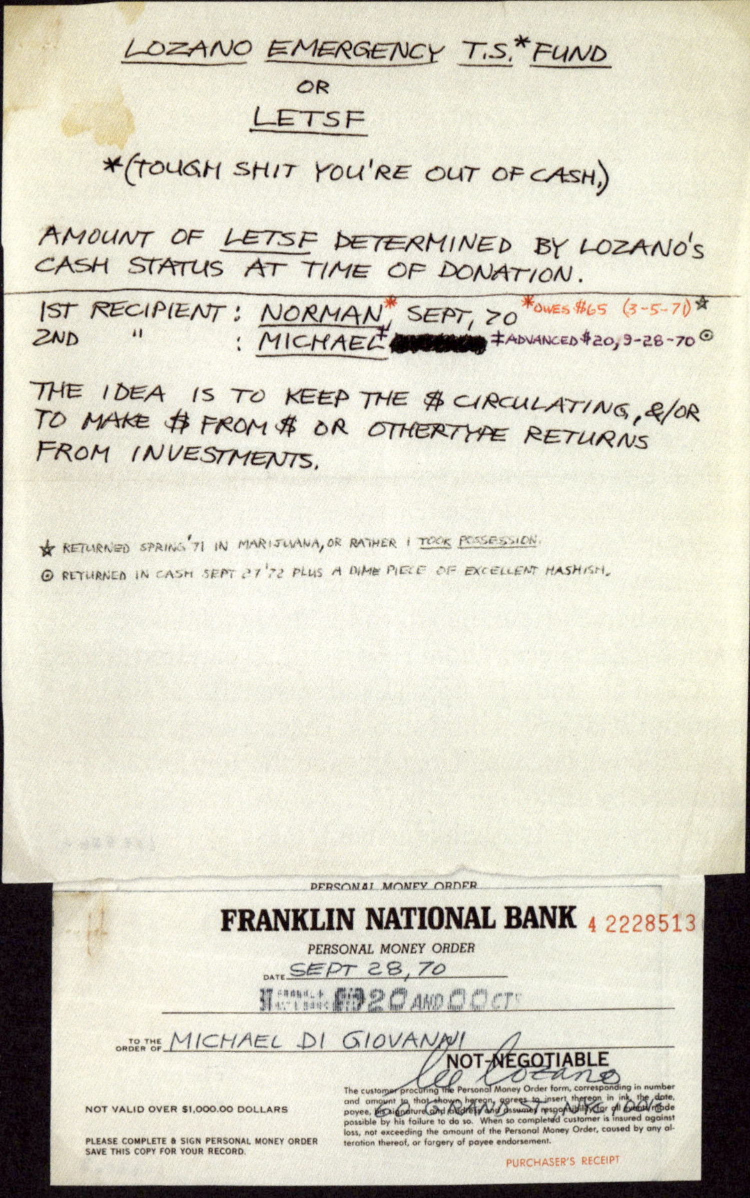

<u>LOZANO EMERGENCY T.S.*FUND</u>

OR

<u>LETSF</u>

*(TOUGH SHIT YOU'RE OUT OF CASH,)

AMOUNT OF <u>LETSF</u> DETERMINED BY LOZANO'S CASH STATUS AT TIME OF DONATION.

IST RECIPIENT : <u>NORMAN</u>* SEPT, 70   *OWES $65 (3-5-71) ☆
2ND   "   : <u>MICHAEL</u> ▬▬▬▬▬ ‡ADVANCED $20, 9-28-70 ◉

THE IDEA IS TO KEEP THE $ CIRCULATING, &/OR TO MAKE $ FROM $ OR OTHERTYPE RETURNS FROM INVESTMENTS.

☆ RETURNED SPRING '71 IN MARIJUANA, OR RATHER I <u>TOOK POSSESSION.</u>

◉ RETURNED IN CASH SEPT 27 '72 PLUS A DIME PIECE OF EXCELLENT HASHISH.

PERSONAL MONEY ORDER

FRANKLIN NATIONAL BANK 4 2228513

PERSONAL MONEY ORDER

DATE SEPT 28, 70

$20 AND 00 CTS

TO THE ORDER OF MICHAEL DI GIOVANNI

NOT-NEGOTIABLE

NOT VALID OVER $1,000.00 DOLLARS

The customer procuring the Personal Money Order form, corresponding in number and amount to that shown hereon, agrees to insert thereon in ink, the date, payee, his signature and address and assumes responsibility for all loss made possible by his failure to do so. When so completed customer is insured against loss, not exceeding the amount of the Personal Money Order, caused by any alteration thereof, or forgery of payee endorsement.

PLEASE COMPLETE & SIGN PERSONAL MONEY ORDER
SAVE THIS COPY FOR YOUR RECORD.

PURCHASER'S RECEIPT

Lozano Emergency T. S. Fund, 1971. Ink on vellum paper with attached money order, 14 × 9¾ in. (35.7 × 24.8 cm)

"The way a junkie looks at his arm"

In the few years preceding Lozano's dropout, the entanglement of her life with her practice seemed to become increasingly inextricable, even for her peers. In a notebook she expressed frustration that Alan Saret referred to her as an "adventuress," accusing her of making art as an "excuse" to pursue her adventures. Lozano's "Life-Art" pieces were not necessarily grand, sensational enterprises. Alongside undoubtedly demanding actions such as *Grass Piece* (p. 31) and *No-Grass Piece* (p. 32), where she spent one month continuously high from smoking marijuana and, in the latter, a shorter period being completely sober, her notebooks reveal rather mundane experiments, such as the *Lie-In-Bed-All-Day-And-Read-Cosmic-Books Piece*, the *Wear-And-Eat-More-Or-Less-The-Same-Thing-Every-Day Piece*, or the *See-How-Long-You-Can-Go-Without-Making-A-Call Piece*.

Lozano sought to test even the most basic routines embedded in the fabric of everyday existence, fascinated by the ways in which habit shapes our behavior. This attitude led her to a sort of experimentation euphoria: "I seem to look at my life the way a junkie looks at his arm," she noted. Eager to investigate anything that could disrupt the conventional order of things, her inquiries often involved the consumption or nonconsumption of drugs, sex, relationships, and emotions, transforming her life into raw material for her work. While many of her peers were beginning to cross the boundary between art and life, Lozano's explorations on the other side of this fence seemed to have brought her farther out, where it was harder to trace her steps back. In a statement published a few years after Lozano's death, Lucy Lippard reflected: "Lee was extraordinarily intense, one of the first, if not the first person (along with Ian Wilson) who did the life-as-art thing. The kind of things other people did as art, she really did as life—and it took us a while to figure that out."

Of Lozano's eighty "Life-Art" pieces, about twenty were transformed into "write-ups," sheets of paper that Lozano would exhibit, or replicate and fax to friends and colleagues. Mostly handwritten, these works were reacting to the Conceptual canon at the time, which prescribed using a typewriter to complete language-based pieces. This choice emphasized the difference between the neutral, distanced speculation of her peers and Lozano's fully engaged, existential involvement in her own pieces. The addressees of these works were ambiguous: written with verbs in the infinitive form, they describe activities Lozano would do (to) herself, while also carrying the potential to function as instructions—an invitation for others to follow her in her endeavors. As with the verb-based titles she had given to her paintings, the infinitive, indicative, and imperative forms overlapped, leaving it to the reader to interpret the action as impersonal, singular, or plural. "Not dictator to anybody, but why not dictator to oneself? Life doesn't seem to be interesting enough when left to 'nature's order.' . . . Why not impose form on one's life the way one makes art? At least it is worth an experiment, and I'm starting now."

  In Pictures

IF I DO THE <u>NO-GRASS PIECE</u>, WHAT WILL HAPPEN TO THE <u>BOOK-OF-CHANGE PIECE</u>?

<u>GRASS PIECE</u>

25   61

MAKE A GOOD SCORE, ABOUT A LID OF EXCELLENT GRASS. SMOKE IT UP AS FAST AS YOU CAN. STAY HIGH ALL DAY, EVERY DAY. SEE WHAT HAPPENS. (APRIL 1, 69)
ONE THING THAT HAPPENS IS THAT IT TAKES MORE AND MORE GRASS TO GET FEELIN GOOD. IMMUNITY BUILDING UP? (APR 17, 69)
THE AMOUNT OF GRASS NEEDED TO GET HIGH HAS STABILIZED ITSELF. TONIGHT I STARTED TO SMOKE THE LAST CONTAINER OF CLEANED SHIT. WHEN THAT IS GONE THERE ARE TWIGS, TO SMOKE AND A LOT OF SEEDS WHICH I AM GOING TO EAT. (THIS HAS BEEN A SCINTILLATING PIECE BUT I'D LIKE TO FINISH IT IN A FLASH.) DECIDED ON NEXT PIECE: GO WITHOUT GRASS FOR THE SAME AMOUNT OF TIME.

> "SEEK THE EXTREMES,
> THAT'S WHERE ALL THE
> ACTION IS."   (APRIL 24, 69)

I GET MORE TIRED EVERY DAY. THIS FEELING WASTED MIGHT BE FROM SMOKING SO MUCH GRASS, OR FROM WORKING SO HARD WHICH I'VE BEEN DOING, OR FROM THE MONOTONOUSNESS OF MY DAYS. (APRIL 23, 69)
I'LL END THE <u>GRASS PIECE</u> WITH A FANFARE: A CAP OF MESCALINE KALTENBACH GAVE ME. (MAY 2, 69)* NOT HIGH ANYMORE, JUST NUMB. FINISHED GRASS, TWIGS & SEEDS. (MAY 3, 69)
*THIS WAS POSTPONED DUE TO CIRCUMSTANCES BEYOND MY CONTROL. FINALLY TOOK MESCALINE: MAY 11, 69. IT BLANKED OUT, MUST'VE BEEN A DUD PILL, A BAD CAP.

<u>NOTE</u>: ASIDE FROM WHEN I WOKE UP (DOWN) IN THE MORNING THERE WERE TWO OCCASIONS WHEN I WASN'T HIGH DURING THIS PIECE, ABOUT A COUPLE OF HOURS EACH. THERE'S A SPOT OF YIN IN EVERY YANG & A SPOT OF YANG IN EVERY YIN, AS "THEY" SAY.

Grass Piece, 1969. Ink on paper with collage, 11 × 8½ in. (28 × 21.5 cm)

NO-GRASS PIECE

GO WITHOUT GRASS FOR THE SAME AMOUNT
OF TIME AS GRASS PIECE, WHICH TURNS
OUT TO BE 33 DAYS. START IMMEDIATELY
AFTER GRASS PIECE. (MAY 4, 69) [PIECE ENDS JUNE 6, 69].
PARANOIA STARTS, (MAY 4, 69) OTHER PRE-GRASS SYMPTOMS.
NOTICE SUCH AN INTENSE FLOW OF ADRENALIN
THAT I GET HIGH ON IT. (MAY 5, 69) GET HIGH
ON A SMALL GLASS OF WINE. (MAY 5, 69)
SLEEPLESS NIGHT, LAST NIGHT ANOTHER PRE-GRASS SYMPTOM. (MAY 6, 69)
EXCESSIVE DREAMING. (MAY 7, 69) HALF-AWAKE DREAMS.
EVERYTHING SEEMS FUNNIER. (MAY 9, 69)
TONIGHT I FELT TENSE & HAD A HEADACHE & WANTED TO
TURN ON FOR THE FIRST TIME IN THIS PIECE. (MAY 9, 69) IF
SOMEONE HAD OFFERED ME GRASS I WOULD'VE TURNED ON.
SLEEPLESSNESS CONTINUES; FITS OF PIQUE. (MAY 10, 69)
UNCONTROLLABLE SADNESS. (MAY 10, 69) DEATHNESS.
DROP MESCALINE BUT IT'S A DUD SO FRIENDS TURN ME ON WITH
HASH & GRASS TO GET ME OFF MY BAD NO-TRIP. (MAY 11, 69)
SLEEPLESSNESS CONTINUES. (MAY 12, 69). A FRIEND WHO
VISITS BRINGS ME A JOINT. HOW CAN I REFUSE? (MAY 12, 69)
SLEEP WELL, LAST NIGHT FOR FIRST TIME SINCE MAY 5. (MAY 14, 69) SMOKING
GRASS WOULD HAVE MADE TODAY SO MUCH BETTER (I AM WAITING
FOR SOMETHING). (MAY 14, 69) SLEEPLESSNESS RETURNS. I LIE
IN BED & GET IDEAS, INSTEAD OF TURNING ON & GETTING IDEAS. (MAY 16, 69)
START A "SEND GRASS TO BOGSIDE" MOVEMENT. [WHAT
CAN YOU DO FOR THE YOUNG BLACKS & P.R.'s TRYING TO
GET AN "EDUCATION" IN N.Y. & ELSEWHERE WHO ALREADY HAVE GRASS?
SEND THEM YOUR NEW ART, (HIGH-INFORMATION ART)]. (MAY 16, 69)
(WRITE THIS UP & SUBMIT IT, MAY 17 WITH GRASS PIECE TO LUCY'S SHOW-MAY 18, 69)
MOOSE VISITS & THEN WE GO OVER TO HIS CRIB & TURN ON
AT MY REQUEST & HAVE A GREAT DIALOGUE. WHEN MOOSE
WAS HERE I ASKED HIM IF HE HAD ANY GRASS & WOULD HE
TURN ME ON. (MAY 17, 69) CAN'T SLEEP. (MAY 19, 69). EXHAUSTION
INCREASES DAILY. (MAY 22, 69) JOHN TORREANO VISITS WITH SOME
DELICIOUS HOME-GROWN IN AN ENVELOPE. WE SHARE SOME
DURING DIALOGUE. HE WISHES TO LEAVE THE REST WITH ME

(CONTINUED ON P. 49)

NOTE: PERHAPS SLEEPLESSNESS IS BECAUSE I DON'T WANT TO DREAM, DURING MY DREAMS I TRAVEL, WHICH IS EXHAUSTING. I DON'T WANT TO GO ANYWHERE RIGHT NOW!

WE SHARE JOINT BUT I DON'T GET VERY HIGH.

No-Grass Piece (part one), 1969. Ink on paper, 11 × 8½ in. (28 × 21.5 cm)

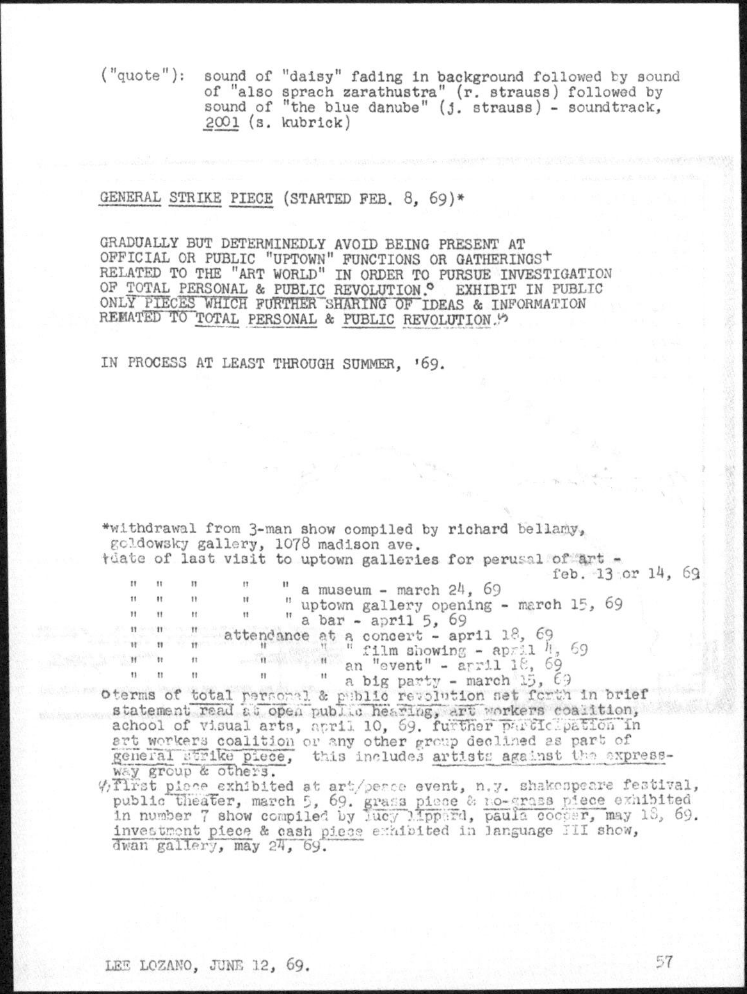

("quote"):   sound of "daisy" fading in background followed by sound
               of "also sprach zarathustra" (r. strauss) followed by
               sound of "the blue danube" (j. strauss) - soundtrack,
               2001 (s. kubrick)

GENERAL STRIKE PIECE (STARTED FEB. 8, 69)*

GRADUALLY BUT DETERMINEDLY AVOID BEING PRESENT AT
OFFICIAL OR PUBLIC "UPTOWN" FUNCTIONS OR GATHERINGS†
RELATED TO THE "ART WORLD" IN ORDER TO PURSUE INVESTIGATION
OF TOTAL PERSONAL & PUBLIC REVOLUTION.°   EXHIBIT IN PUBLIC
ONLY PIECES WHICH FURTHER SHARING OF IDEAS & INFORMATION
REMATED TO TOTAL PERSONAL & PUBLIC REVOLUTION.↳

IN PROCESS AT LEAST THROUGH SUMMER, '69.

*withdrawal from 3-man show compiled by richard bellamy,
 goldowsky gallery, 1078 madison ave.
†date of last visit to uptown galleries for perusal of art -
                                        feb. 13 or 14, 69
     "   "   "   "   " a museum - march 24, 69
     "   "   "   "   " uptown gallery opening - march 15, 69
     "   "   "   "   " a bar - april 5, 69
     "   "   "   attendance at a concert - april 18, 69
     "   "   "   "   " " film showing - april 4, 69
     "   "   "   "   " " an "event" - april 18, 69
     "   "   "   "   " " a big party - march 15, 69
°terms of total personal & public revolution set forth in brief
 statement read at open public hearing, art workers coalition,
 school of visual arts, april 10, 69. further participation in
 art workers coalition or any other group declined as part of
 general strike piece, this includes artists against the express-
 way group & others.
↳first piece exhibited at art/peace event, n.y. shakespeare festival,
 public theater, march 5, 69. grass piece & no-grass piece exhibited
 in number 7 show compiled by lucy lippard, paula cooper, may 18, 69.
 investment piece & cash piece exhibited in language III show,
 dwan gallery, may 24, 69.

LEE LOZANO, JUNE 12, 69.   57

General Strike Piece, 1969. Offset ink on paper, 11 × 8½ in. (28 × 21.7 cm)

QUOTE, LETTER FROM MICHAEL, SEPT 20, 70: "INFO - SEND ME YOUR MASTURBATION PIECE - OR DETAILS ABOUT IT."

MASTURBATION INVESTIGATION (APRIL 3-5, #69)

NOTE: OTHER PIECES SIMULTANEOUSLY IN PROCESS: GRASS PIECE, GENERAL STRIKE PIECE, & A WITHDRAWAL FROM HUMANS & THE OUTSIDE WORLD. I REFUSE TO SEE MY PARTNER OR ANYONE ELSE.

APR 3: MASTURBATION TO FANTASIES: BALLING SPECIFIC HUMANS, THEN IMAGINARY HUMANS.

MASTURBATION TO PICTURES: SCREW, ISSUES 9 & 10.

APR 4: MASTURBATION USING VARIOUS OBJECTS: HARD RUBBER MOTORCYCLE PEDAL, FEATHER, CARROT,* PHALLIC-SHAPED LIGHTBULB.

APR 5: MASTURBATION LOOKING INTO SMALL MIRROR REFLECTING GENITAL: OBSERVE TUMESCENCE, TURGIDITY, COLOR CHANGE FROM LIGHT RED TO BRIGHT RED, VIOLENT EJACULATION OF LUBRICATION FROM DUCT NEAR CLITORIS, & VIBRATION DURING ORGASM.

SATISFACTION OF INTEREST IN INVESTIGATING MASTURBATION.

* IT WAS A SEXY CARROT & BEING ████████████ ORGANIC, WORKED BEST OF ALL THE OBJECTS USED. BUT BALLIN' WITH OBJECTS IS THE ABYSS.

CC - MICHAEL, % MORNING SUN FARM.

Masturbation Investigation, 1969. Carbon paper transfer on paper, 11 × 8½ in.

PARTY PIECE (OR PARANOIA PIECE)

DESCRIBE YOUR CURRENT WORK TO A FAMOUS BUT FAILING ARTIST FROM THE EARLY 60's. WAIT TO SEE WHETHER HE BOOSTS* ANY OF YOUR IDEAS. (MARCH 15, 69)
*HOIST, COP, STEAL

PAINTING PIECE

NOW I REALIZE THAT THE WAVE SERIES MUST BE KEPT PRIVATE, WITHIN THE STUDIO, TO BE AVAILABLE ONLY TO THOSE PEOPLE I LIKE ENOUGH TO INVITE OVER, OR THOSE WHO HAVE THE CHUTZPAH TO COME UN-INVITED. (APRIL 3, 69) MAKE ANOTHER KIND OF ART FOR THE OUTSIDE WORLD.

REAL MONEY PIECE

OFFER TO GUESTS COFFEE, DIET PEPSI, BOURBON, GLASS OF HALF AND HALF, ICE WATER, GRASS, AND MONEY. OPEN JAR OF REAL MONEY AND OFFER IT TO GUESTS LIKE CANDY. (APR 4, 69)

NOTE: APR 3 - OFFER MONEY VERBALLY TO STEVE KALTENBACH. HE REFUSES.
APR 4 - OFFER JAR OF MONEY TO HANNA WEINER. SHE TAKES (BY CHANCE) A $10, WHICH SHE KEEPS. THIS IS A "CHAIN PIECE", SINCE HANNA MUST MAKE A PIECE BY DECIDING WHAT TO DO WITH THE $10. THIS REAL MONEY PIECE HAS BECOME EXCEEDINGLY INTERESTING TO ME. THIS IS A JARRING PIECE.
APR 15 - OFFER JAR TO RON NLEEMAN WHO TAKES OUT A $20. HE WISHES TO PUT IT BACK INTO JAR BUT I TALK HIM INTO KEEPING IT.
APR 17 - KEITH SONNIER REFUSED, LATER SCREWS LID VERY TIGHTLY BACK ON JAR.
APR 27 - KALTENBACH TAKES ALL THE MONEY OUT OF JAR WHEN I OFFER IT, EXAMINES ALL THE MONEY & PUTS IT ALL BACK IN JAR. SAYS HE DOESN'T NEED MONEY NOW.

NOTE: AT BEGINNING OF THIS PIECE THE JAR CONTAINS BILLS OF $5, $10, $20, ABOUT ?$585.'S WORTH, COILED IN TWO OR THREE PACKETS AROUND THE INSIDE OF THE JAR, UNBOUND. THE MONEY COMES FROM ROLF RICKE FROM SALE OF PAINTING "SWITCH".

Party Piece (or Paranoia Piece), Painting Piece, Real Money Piece (part one), 1969. Ink on paper, 11 × 8½ in. (27.9 × 21.6 cm)

<u>REAL MONEY PIECE</u> (CONTINUED)

MORE BILLS ADDED TO JAR (CK FOR $500 FROM PAUL BIANCHINI, SALE OF DRAWINGS, CASHED & ADDED MAY 17,69) INCLUDING $1 BILLS & ONE $100 BILL.

APR 28 — DAVID PARSON REFUSED, LAUGHING.

MAY 1 — WARREN C. INGERSOLL REFUSED. HE GOT <u>VERY</u> <u>UPSET</u> ABOUT MY "ATTITUDE TOWARDS MONEY."

MAY 4 — KEITH SONNIER REFUSED, BUT SAID HE WOULD TAKE MONEY IF HE NEEDED IT WHICH HE MIGHT IN NEAR FUTURE.

MAY 7 — DICK ANDERSON BARELY GLANCES AT THE MONEY WHEN I STICK IT UNDER HIS NOSE AND SAYS "OH NO THANKS, I INTEND TO EARN IT ON MY OWN."

MAY 8 — BILLY [BRYANT CONLEY] DIDN'T TAKE ANY BUT THEN IT WAS SORT OF SPOILED BECAUSE I HAD TOLD HIM ABOUT THIS PIECE ON THE PHONE & HE HAD TIME TO THINK ABOUT IT HE SAID.

MAY 10 — DAN GRAHAM PUTS $50 INTO THE JAR (TO REPAY LOAN).

MAY 12 — ABE LUBELSKI REFRAINS, SAYS HE'S EXPECTING A BIG CHECK SOON, INCOME TAX RETURN (I THINK).

MAY 13 — PAUL BIANCHINI DECLINES UNTIL HE CAN "ASK HIS WIFE," THEN ASKS ME WHY I HAVE MONEY IN A <u>BROWN</u> JAR. SIMONNE STERN (WHO HAS A GALLERY IN NEW ORLEANS) SAYS SHE DOESN'T CARE TO HAVE ANY NOW, "TOO SALTY."

MAY 15 — DAN GRAHAM TAKES $30 FROM JAR (ON LOAN).

MAY 16 — ROLF & USCHI [RICKE] VISIT. USCHI TAKES OUT BILL ($20) & ROLF TAKES NEXT BILL ($5). I URGE THEM TO KEEP MONEY, WHICH THEY STASH IN THEIR WALLETS AFTER A WHILE.

MAY 17 — OFFER MONEY (ONLY $25 LEFT IN JAR) TO MOOSE, HE DOESN'T TAKE ANY.

<u>WRITE UP PIECE</u> FOR ~~POSSIBLE~~ <u>INCLUSION IN DWAN LANGUAGE SHOW.</u> (MAY 19, 69)

MAY 20 — DAVID LEE TAKES $1. [<u>NOTE</u>: START NEW METHOD OF FIRST REMOVING <u>ALL</u> BILLS FROM JAR, SPREADING THEM OUT & OFFERING FREE CHOICE OF VARIOUS DENOMINATIONS: "DECK OF CARDS" METHOD.]

MAY 22 — JOHN TORREANO DOESN'T ~~TAKE~~ WANT ANY MONEY (SAYS HE DOESN'T NEED IT NOW ~~REALLY~~) BUT HE TAKES THE JAR! HOORAY!

" 23 — PAULA DAVIES & MARILYN LEARNER DROP IN UNEXPECTEDLY. NEITHER TAKES ANY LACE BUT PAULA SAYS LATER SHE WAS "CONTROLLING HERSELF."

" 25 — ALAN SARET TAKES ALL THE MONEY FOR A MINUTE BUT I MUST HAVE HAD AN EXPRESSION OF TERROR ON MY FACE BECAUSE HE PUTS IT ALL BACK.

<u>REAL MONEY PIECE</u> (CONT.)

MAY 26,69 — LARRY WEINER TAKES $1.

" 26 — DAN VISITS TO BORROW #10. THAT MAKES #40 HE OWES "JAR".

" 28 — CLAIRE COPLEY DOESN'T TAKE ANY, SHE SEEMS INSULTED & OFFENDED
THAT I OFFER IT TO HER (IN SUCH A 'VULGAR' WAY?).

JUNE 3 — BRICE MARDEN DOESN'T NEED ANY, HE SAYS, & FINDS IT AMUSING, LAUGHS.

" 6 — ALAN SARET VISITS AGAIN & MAKES A <u>PIECE</u> OF THE MONEY
WHICH IS NOW IN TWO PILES ON THE FLOOR, EACH SHAPED
SIMILARLY TO A "FOOTSTEP" BY FOLDING & MOLDING TO HIS
HAND. IT LOOKS GOOD LIKE THAT & I'M GONNA LEAVE
IT ON THE FLOOR FOR A WHILE.

JUNE 16 — GARY BOWER DOESN'T TAKE ANY NOW BUT SAYS HE MIGHT
COME BACK FOR SOME IN A FEW DAYS.

" 17 — GARY STEVENS PLAYS W/MONEY, RESTACKS IT, COUNTS IT?,
DOESN'T TAKE ANY.

" 23 — FOR SOME REASON I JUST DON'T FEEL LIKE OFFERING
LACE TO FELIX ROTH.

" 24 — JAKE ASKS IF HE CAN TAKE $10 TO COVER ACID IN
ADVANCE & OF COURSE I GIVE IT TO HIM. (JULY 1, 69 —
JAKE RETNS $10 BECAUSE HE CAN'T SCORE NOW).

JULY 1 — JAKE AND/OR BRIAN SUBSTITUTE A $1 BILL FOR A $20 BILL
WHEN I AM NOT LOOKING. I GUESS IT WAS <u>BRIAN</u>, WHO
ASKED ME FOR MONEY IN RETN FOR DRAWING HE LEFT
HERE TO WHICH I REPLIED THAT I'D RATHER HE STEAL
IT THAN ASK ME FOR IT. DISCOVER SUBSTITUTION AFTER THEY LEAVE.

JUNE 30 — NOR DO I OFFER IT TO ROMY McDONALD & FRIEND MARGO
FROM ENGLAND, ALTO I TELL THEM ABT THE <u>PIECE</u>.

JULY 9,69 — JASON CRUM REFUSES TO TAKE MONEY.

" 9, " — ARTHUR BERMAN WHO IS FLAT BROKE WILL ONLY
TAKE 20¢ FOR HIS SUBWAY FARE HOME.

Party Piece (or Paranoia Piece), Painting Piece, Real Money Piece (part three), 1969.
Ink on paper, 11 × 8½ in. (27.9 × 21.6 cm)

FEB. 28, 69
DRAWING FOR LUCY'S <u>PEACE SHOW</u>

<u>PIECE</u>:

WHEN YOU'RE "TRYING TO MAKE IT" KEEP GOING FOR YEARS A PILE OF SHOW ANNOUNCEMENTS, PRESS RELEASE MATERIAL, ALL PRINTED MATTER RELATING TO THE ART SCENE. EVERYTHING THAT COMES IN THE MAIL OR IS ACCUMULATED OTHER WAYS IS TOSSED ON THE PILE. WHEN YOU "START TO MAKE IT" THROW YOUR OWN PRINTED MATTER ON THE PILE. LET IT BE COVERED UP BY TIME THE WAY EVERYBODY ELSE'S IS.

<u>COMPANION PIECE</u>:

TOSS YOUR OWN PRINTED MATTER ON TOP OF THE PILE AND KEEP IT ON TOP OF THE PILE.

LEE LOZANO

LEE LOZANO   60 GRAND ST.   N.Y.C. 10013

(QUOTE) – BLOW YR NOSE TO BREATHE CLEARLY. BLOW YR MIND TO THINK CLEARLY.

CLARIFICATION PIECE (JULY 28, 69)

MAKE A CLEAR DISTINCTION‡ BETWEEN A PIECE AS AN ACT OR SERIES (SET) OF ACTS IN TIME, & THE WRITE-UP✳ OF A PIECE WHICH OCCURS ONLY WHEN THERE IS OCCASION TO SHOW THE WRITE-UP (EITHER PUBLICLY OR PRIVATELY IN THE FORM USUALLY OF LETTERS TO INDIVIDUALS).

FIRST WRITE-UP OF A PIECE : DRAWING✳ FOR LUCY'S PEACE SHOW (FEB 28, 69).

SOME EARLY PIECES† EITHER WRITTEN UP LATER OR NOT YET WRITTEN UP:

THE JAN 1, 68 TO DEC 31, 69 OR 70 PIECE✂ INFO FOR THIS PIECE WAS BEGUN TO BE COLLECTED ON JAN 1, 68.

INVESTMENT PIECE (JAN 15, 69). INITIATED AS A PIECE & DESCRIBED VERBALLY AS A PIECE FROM DATE OF INVESTMENT (JAN 15, 69) TO DATE OF WRITE-UP (FOR DWAN LANGUAGE III SHOW, MAY 19, 69).

PILE YOUR READING MATERIAL PIECE (BEGUN AS INTEREST IN ALREADY EXISTING ACCRETION INCREASED, ABT EARLY 68). DESCRIBED VERBALLY AS A PIECE DURING 68.

TV PIECE (APRIL 13, 68 TO JULY 9, 68).

NIGHT SKY SHOW PIECE (APR 11, 68). DESCRIBED VERBALLY AS A PIECE TO BE IMAGINED, 68 & 69.

ETC.

‡ TO MARCIA TUCKER AFTER DIALOGUE JULY 28, 69.
✳ ALL WRITE-UPS OF PIECES ARE DRAWINGS. ← PLEASE NOTE!✹
† SOMETIMES CALLED INVESTIGATIONS. OR EXPERIMENTS.
✂ SUBJECT TO REMAIN UNDISCLOSED UNTIL COMPLETION.
✹ THIS IS THE DISTINCTION BETWEEN A ONE-OF-A-KIND° (HAND) PRINTED (PIECE OF) MATTER & PRINTED MATTER, WHICH IS ▓▓▓ REPRODUCED MATTER.
° I GOTTA ALLOW A FEW CARBON COPIES. OR ZEROX COPIES.

Clarification Piece, 1969. Carbon paper transfer with ink and colored pencil on paper, 11 × 8 in. (27.9 × 20.3 cm)

An undated note of Lozano's exploring different names

Identity Is a Vector

One of the first societal conventions Lozano refuted
was her own name. Born Lenore Knaster, she changed
it for the first time as a teenager in 1944, choosing
Lee as a "rejection of the traditional American middle-
class female trip." She next morphed into Lee Lozano,
following her marriage to architect Adrian Lozano
in 1956. She chose to keep his surname after their
divorce in 1960, perhaps in order to avoid confusion
with painter Lenore "Lee" Krasner, Jackson Pollock's
wife, or perhaps in an effort to further conceal her
roots. The androgynous abbreviation "Lee" lingered for
a while, as did her conflict with the conventional identity
of "woman." In the predominantly male-dominated art
world of the 1960s, it was undeniably convenient for
an artist not to read as female on exhibition invitations
and in the press. In the years following 1970, "Lozano

(the name) snapped off," and she briefly asked to be called Lee Free, then Leefer, then Eefer. "Redesign yourself to suit yourself," she would say, questioning the construction of identity to the point of stripping her own away, one convention at a time, one letter at a time. In the 1980s she finally settled on "E," the minimum possible sound to be pronounced in order to address her, adding that she wanted nothing more to do with "the L universe" anymore. As far as we know, she signed herself as "E" until the end of her life. It is not by chance that the only remaining letter of her name was the one scientists use to indicate "energy," one of her long-lasting obsessions. Yet, in the very end, energy ran out, as did the letters of her name: her last instructions were for her body to be buried in an unmarked grave in Southland Memorial Park in Grand Prairie, Texas. Her dropout was complete and, like many of her works, untitled.

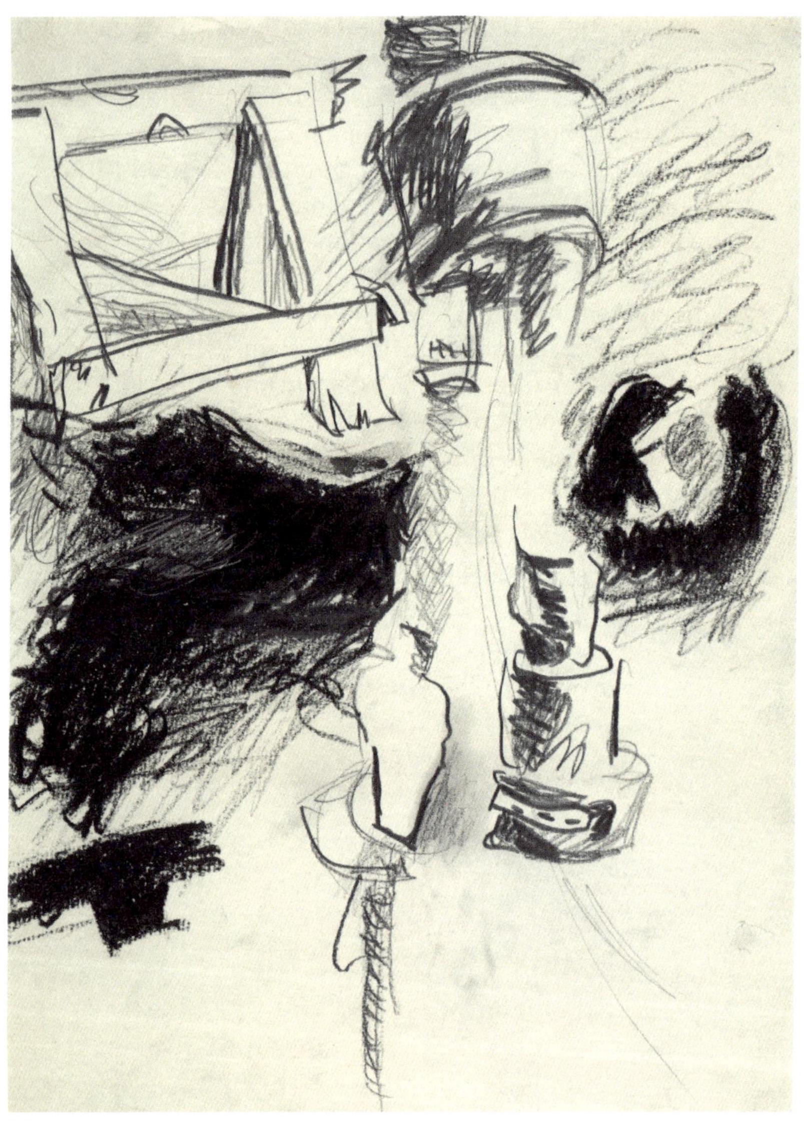

No title, 1961. Graphite on paper, 18⅛ × 13½ in. (46 × 34.2 cm)

The Asshole of N.Y.

When she first arrived in New York, Lozano landed a studio
at 53 West Twenty-Fourth Street. She spent a couple of years
there before moving downtown, first to a loft on Greene
Street and later to Grand Street. She was drawn closer
and closer to Canal Street, or "anal street," as she called it
in one of her drawings from 1964, crossing out the "C" to
better identify the area as the rear end of the city. At the
time, SoHo was a cheap, chaotic, and notoriously sordid
neighborhood, its streets cluttered with the remnants of
years of industrial activity, to eventually be displaced in
favor of gentrification. Lozano would roam the streets,
sometimes in the company of Carl Andre, rummaging
through the city's detritus, picking up items she thought
were worthy of a second chance. She would return to

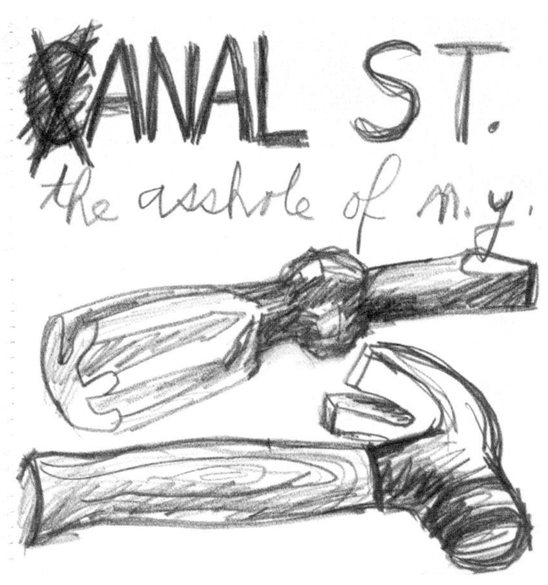

No title, 1964. Graphite on paper, 9 × 9¼ in. (23 × 23.5 cm)

her studio with a loot of variously sized screws, springs, bolts, and other, trickier-to-identify objects, which would sometimes be integrated directly into her work. A found wooden toilet seat later served as a base for one of her signature grinning mouths, holding a turd-like cigar between its teeth (p. 49), the perfect coronation of her scatological pun about Canal Street being "the asshole of N.Y."

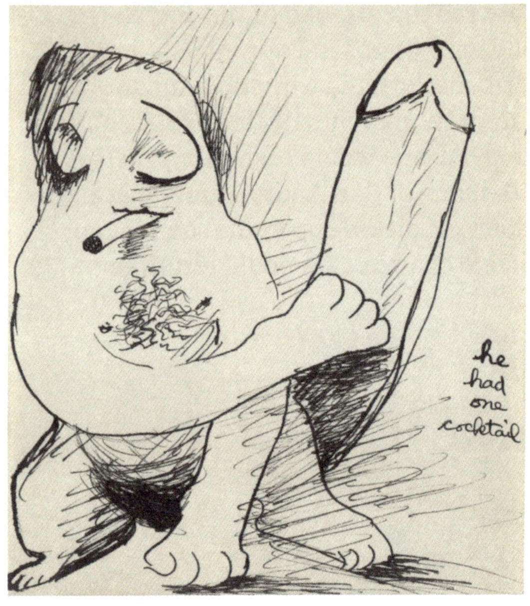

No title, 1962. Ink on paper, 9½ × 8⅝ in. (24 × 21.9 cm)

During Lozano's early years in the city, the permeability of her studio—its openness to the objects she brought in from outside—played a crucial role in shaping her drawings and paintings. The scraps and machinery she scavenged from the streets found their way into her study of the human body, which was rapidly evolving from the classical academic depiction of nude figures into fragmented, oddly scattered pieces of broken bodies, eager to engage with the world

Materials and Making

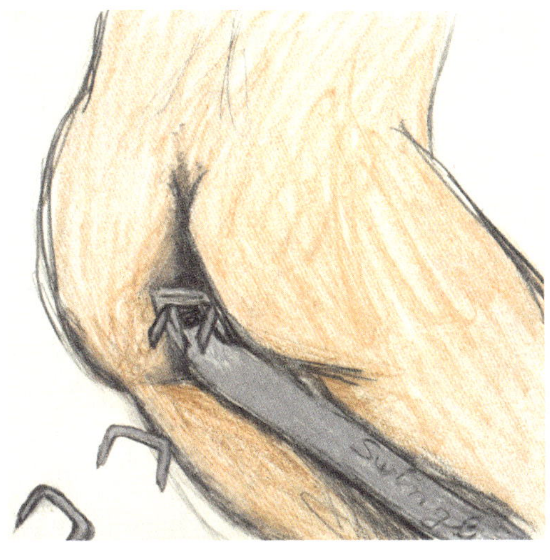

No title, 1963.
Crayon and graphite
on paper, 9 × 9½ in.
(23 × 24 cm)

around them. A vagina reimagined as an electrical plug
ready to receive a toaster; an ass transformed into a stapler;
a penis turned into a slingshot launching a mouthed boob
on fire. And then, cocks: cocks coming out of pockets, ears,
guns, or boxes. Cocks replacing noses and noses replaced
by cocks, cocks morphing into crayons or wrenches,
twofold hybrid boob-cock creatures, cocks disguised
as the disproportionate tails of animal-looking men—
"he had one cocktail," the caption explains.

Magnified or mocked, defaced or severed, the penis was
a central subject in Lozano's visual vocabulary as late as
1964. The portrayal of male genitalia was not a particularly
palatable subject in the visual arts at the time, and, indeed,
the roots of these drawings might be better sought in two
minor genres of visual culture: pornography and satire.
Lozano's drawings depict fiercely crude intercourses—
polymorphous fucking sessions in which sexual norms
are disrupted and dismissed. In these works, not only do

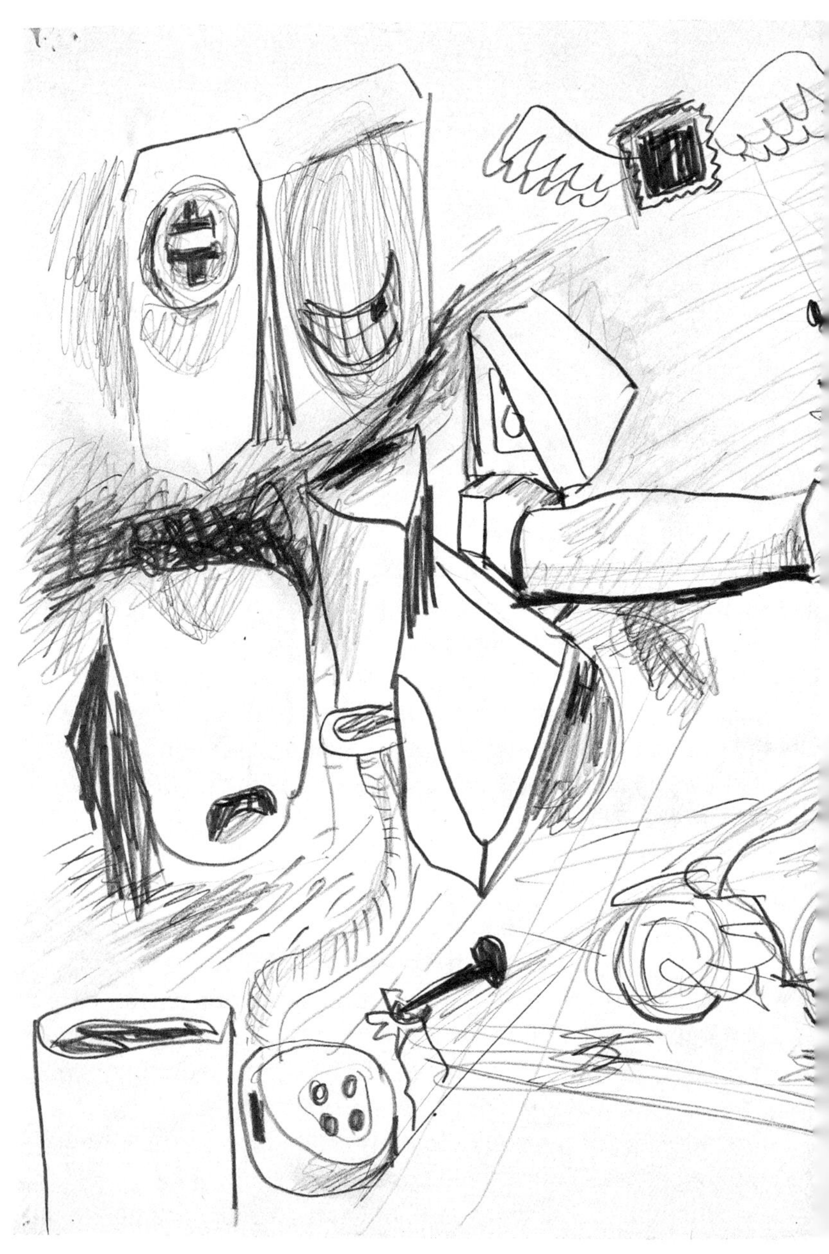

No title, 1961. Graphite and colored pencil on paper, 17³⁄₈ × 22¹⁄₂ in. (44.2 × 57.1 cm)

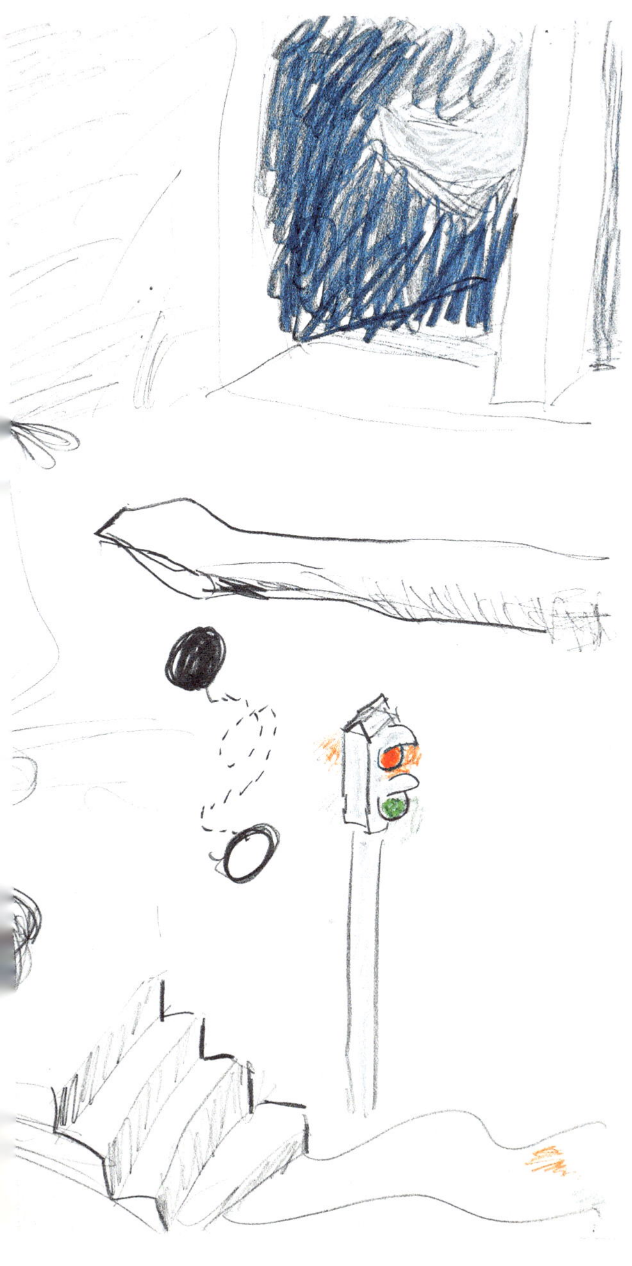

traditional gender norms and conventional passive/active roles fail to apply, but the very functions of bodies and objects are transgressed, deviated, and perverted into grotesque choreographies where even the laws of physics are spectacularly defied. The penis, at first glance the undisputed protagonist of the scene, upon closer analysis appears as a vigorous yet domesticated actor, devoid of its own willpower. In most drawings, it is violently separated from its owner and transformed by Lozano into an array of other possible objects: cocks become tools like any other, used—not necessarily with consent—to satisfy someone else's pleasure.

Years later, in 1969, Lozano's onanistic fantasies materialized in a piece titled *Masturbation Investigation* (p. 34), a three-day experiment that aptly coincided with *Grass Piece* and *General Strike Piece*. As part of her investigations, Lozano masturbated to fantasies of "specific humans," then to "imaginary humans," and finally to images found in the magazine *Screw*. Using a small mirror, she observed her genitals during both masturbation and orgasm, noting changes in color, turgidity, and lubrication. She experimented with various objects, including a hard rubber motorcycle pedal, a feather, a carrot (which she declared "the most effective" tool), and a phallic-shaped light bulb. These experiments, along with Lozano's earlier explicit drawings, reflect her departure from an androcentric vision of sexuality. Even when engaging with partners and meticulously documenting each sexual encounter— noting the frequency and quality of her orgasms—Lozano's exploration of sexuality remains a fundamentally solipsistic and autocratic project. It is characterized by replacement and multiplication rather than exclusivity, driven by manipulation rather than worship.

                    Materials and Making

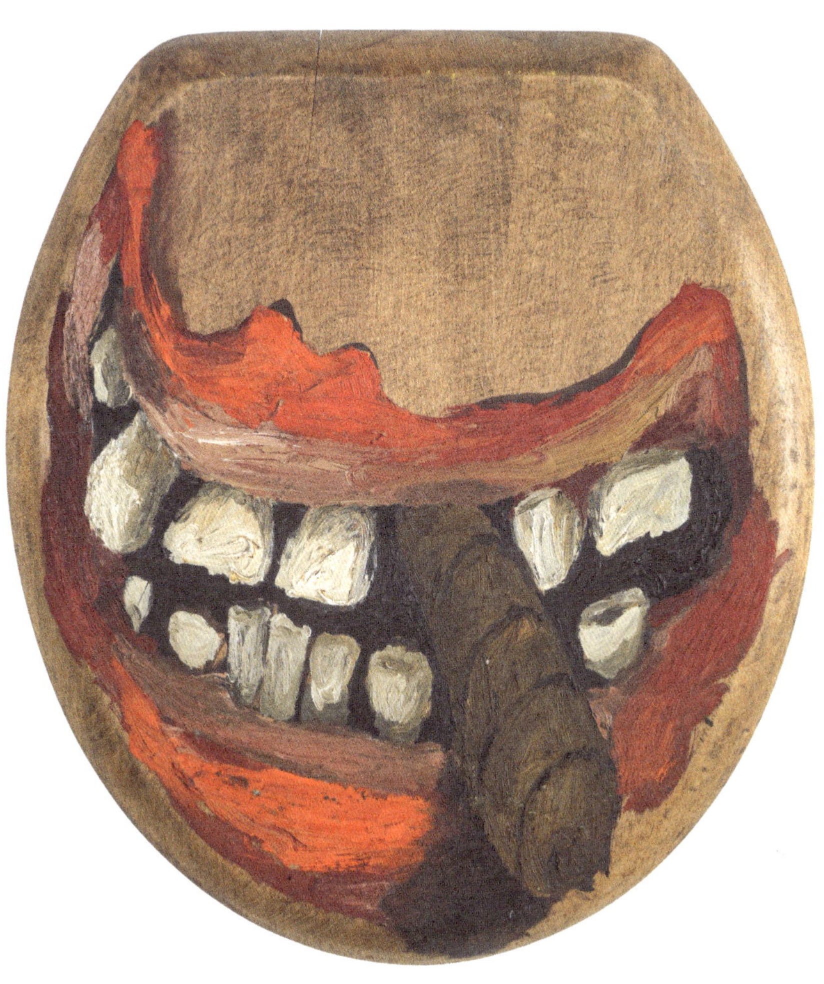

No title, 1962–63. Oil on wood toilet seat, 14¾ × 13¼ × ¾ in. (37.5 × 33.5 × 2 cm)

"Note drawn with real shit"

Despite its obvious "pun-value," shit was a serious matter for Lozano. Her interest in organic by-products and bodily excretions was not only driven by an obsession with the functions and dysfunctions of the body (especially her own) but also tied to her reflections on painting. While commenting on her frenemy Robert Morris's landmark 1968 *Artforum* article "Anti Form," Lozano fiercely distanced herself from the work of Jackson Pollock and Morris Louis, who she referred to as "Moose's current two painter heroes." According to Morris, by dripping or pouring paint directly onto the canvas, these artists acknowledged the inherent tendencies and properties of paint as liquid matter, thereby aligning with his critique of formalism in favor of process and materiality. Lozano, however, proposed a different category for her own work: "another concept of paint is its being matter in a <u>solid</u> state. A painter who thinks of it this way is Lee Lozano, whose bowels function magnificently." Lozano satirizes and counters Abstract Expressionism's liquid-centric vision by presenting paint as solid fecal matter. This dichotomy is further explored in her early canvases, where earwax, pus, secretions, mucus, and discharge are often depicted as if directly placed on the canvas. The metaphorical identification of paint with bodily excretions reaches its peak in a small-scale ink drawing in which the subject is partially covered by a brown mark in colored pencil. The scene is captioned by the artist: "note drawn with real shit."

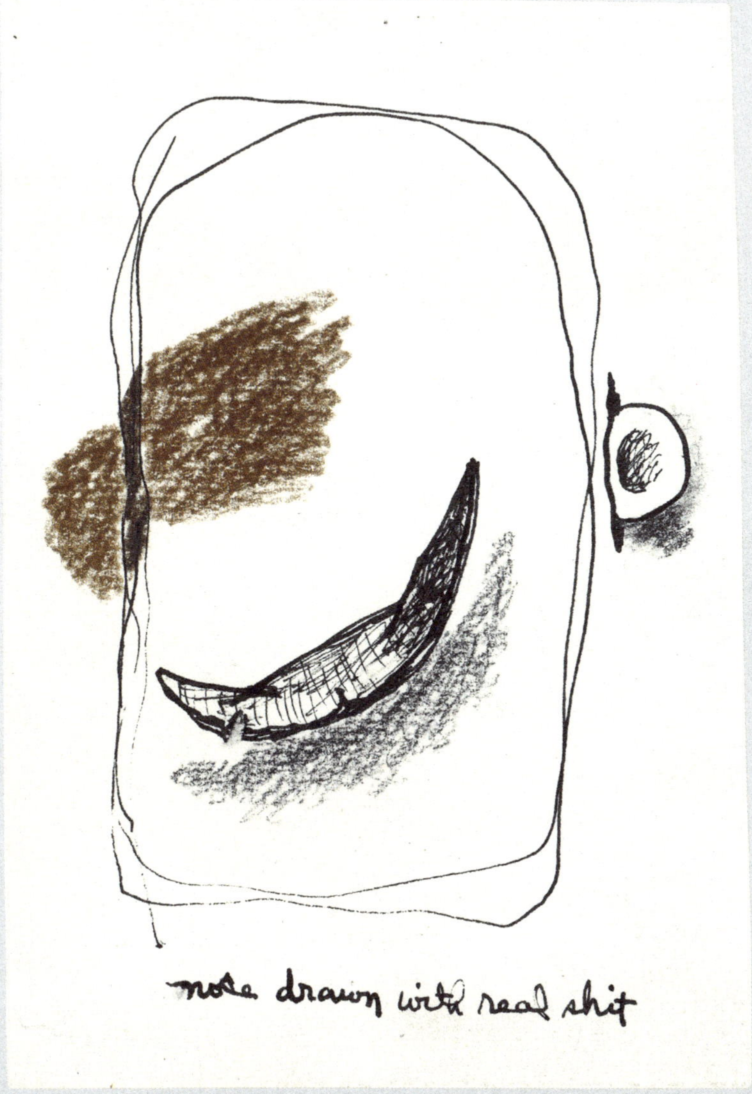

No title, 1962. Ink and colored pencil on paper, 7 × 5 in. (17.9 × 12.7 cm)

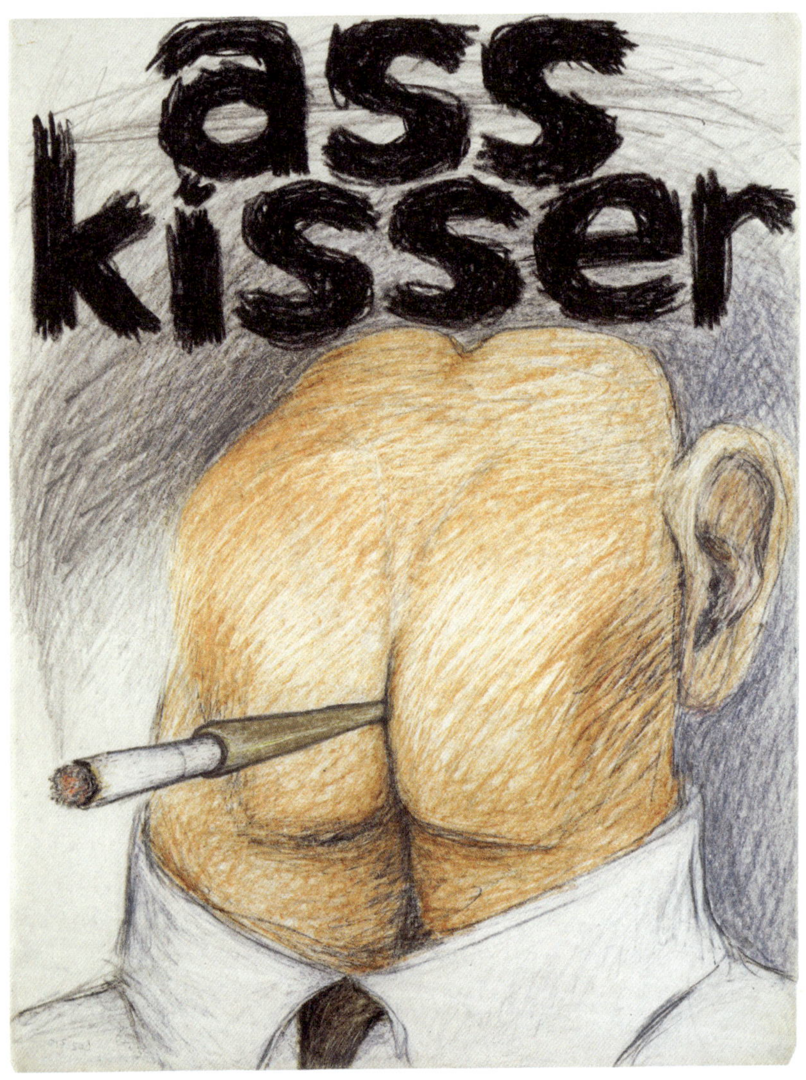

No title, 1962. Crayon on paper, 23½ × 18 in. (60 × 46 cm)

Pun Value

Despite Lozano's enthusiastic research into sexuality, when looking at the drawings she made between 1960 and 1964, her ultimate objective doesn't seem to be orgasmic but, rather, outrageously humoristic. In her work, the penis often stands for something else, usually something that needs to be made fun of, as a symbol of the male-dominated world she was living in. The comical and critical purpose of Lozano's drawings reveals their genealogy, since trivializing society's power relations through obscene imagery—in order to undermine them—is a classic tool of satire. The cartoonish quality of the drawings also recalls newspaper comic strips, pointing again to a tradition that deploys explicit motifs as a scandalous tool to elicit amusement, but also political concern.

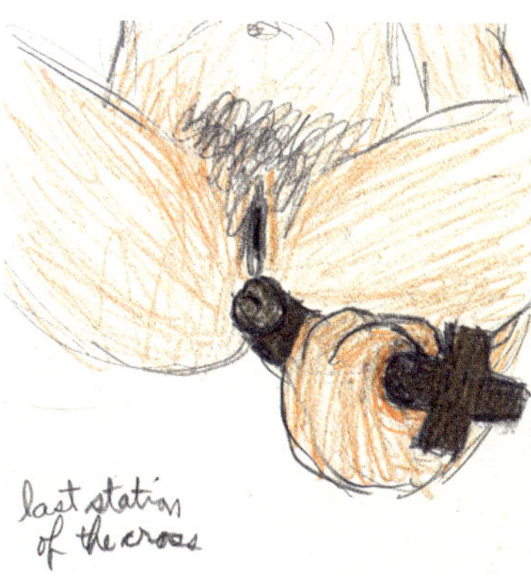

No title, 1963. Graphite and crayon on paper, 9½ × 9 in. (24.2 × 22.8 cm)

Lozano's satirical arsenal spared no one, taking particular aim at institutions and their conventional symbols. Her blasphemous imagery targeted religion, with cock rings shaped like the Star of David and crosses morphing into erect penises, one of which is held by a character poised to insert it into her vagina, labeled "last station of the cross." Formal education is ridiculed in a drawing in which a penis transforms into a flaccid tassel on a graduation mortarboard—possibly a nod to Lozano's own graduation, when she appeared onstage

to receive her diploma with her graduation gown tangled in
her bra, which was not worn on her breasts, but instead hung
out of her jean's back pocket. The nationalistic history of
the United States is not spared, with the timber rattlesnake
of the Gadsden flag, a symbol of the American Revolution
later co-opted by conservative right-wing movements,
reimagined as a long, slithering penis (p. 59).

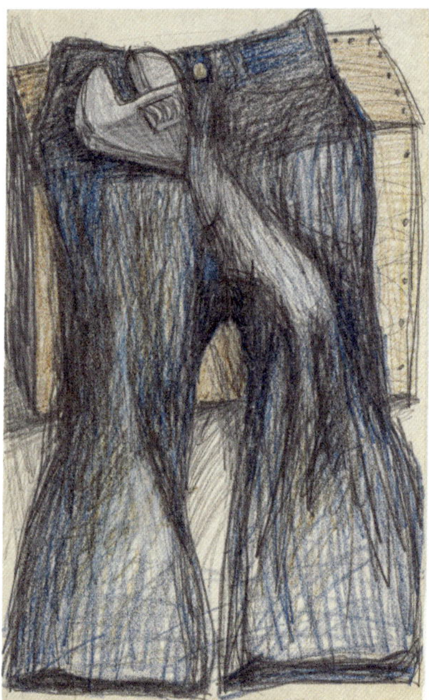

No title, 1963.
Graphite, colored
pencil, and crayon
on paper, 23 × 14½ in.
(58.5 × 36.8 cm)

White-collar workers are satirized in drawings in
which the top of a suit is crowned not by a face but by
an ass ("asskisser") or a penis ("cockhead"). Blue-collar
workers are also targeted, as seen in a depiction of a metal
wrench protruding from the open fly of a worker's jeans.
The image could be interpreted as a jab at the macho
workshop labor aesthetic embraced at the time by fellow

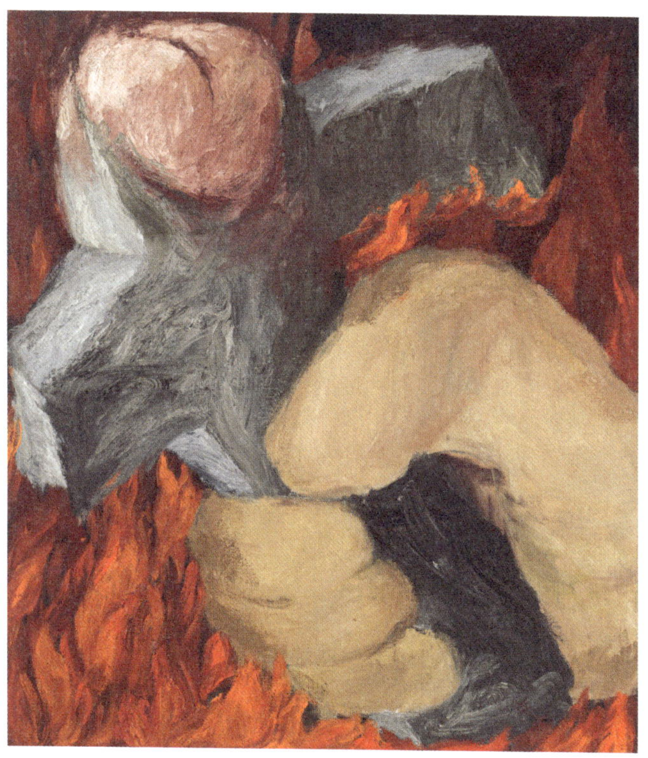

No title, 1962. Oil on canvas, 36 × 31¾ in. (91.4 × 80.7 cm)

artists Robert Morris, Carl Andre, and Richard Serra.
In some instances, Lozano's dysfunctional bodies are
paired with dysfunctional machines, ultimately pointing
to the broader dysfunctionality of society as a whole.
One drawing declares, "I got fucked in the (g)ass by
ConEdison," (p. 56) a pun on "gas" and "ass" directed at her
energy provider. The drawing features a grinning, eyeless
character whose nose extends into a long-reach lighter
tipped with a blue flame. In the background, household
appliances are crammed together as dull, passive bystanders
to the caustic joke.

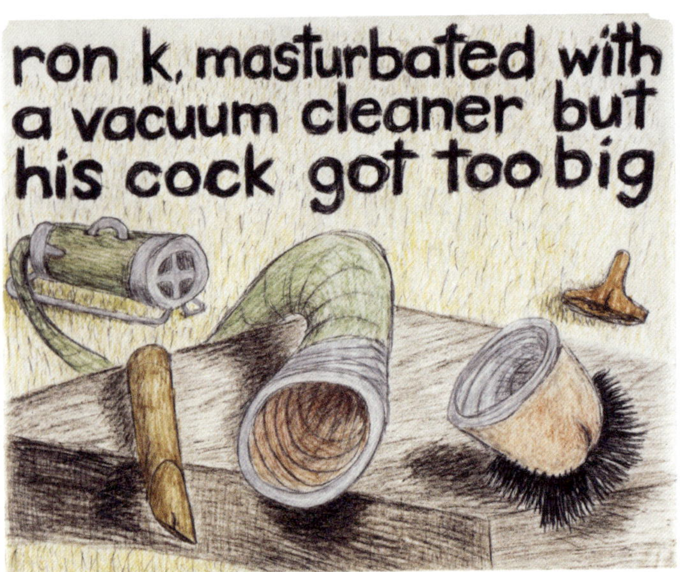

No title, 1962. Graphite and crayon on paper, 18¾ × 23⅞ in. (47.6 × 60.5 cm)

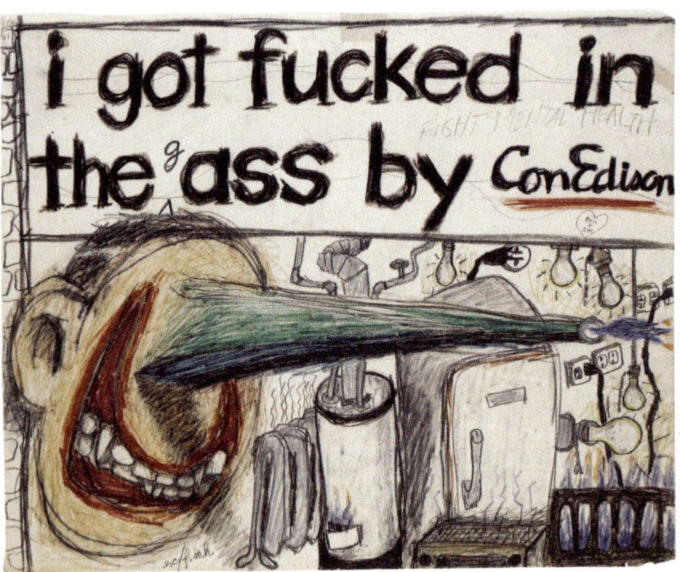

No title, 1962. Graphite and crayon on paper, 18¾ × 23¾ in. (47.6 × 60.3 cm)

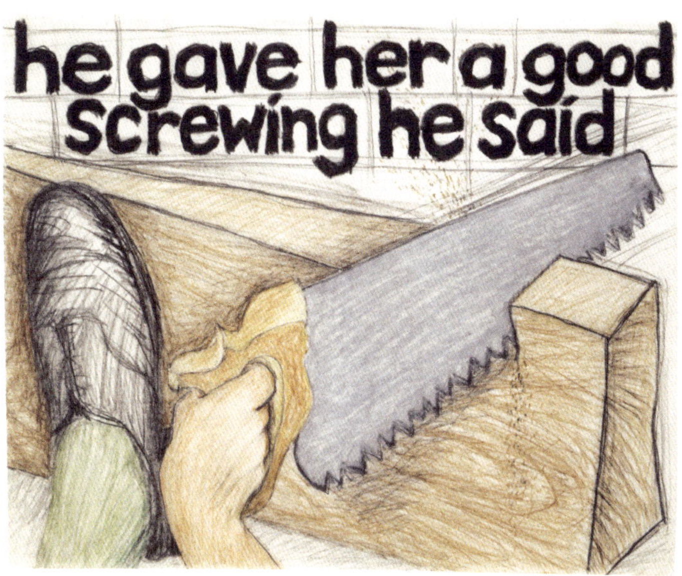

No title, 1962. Colored pencil and crayon on paper, 18¾ × 23⅞ in. (47.6 × 60.5 cm)

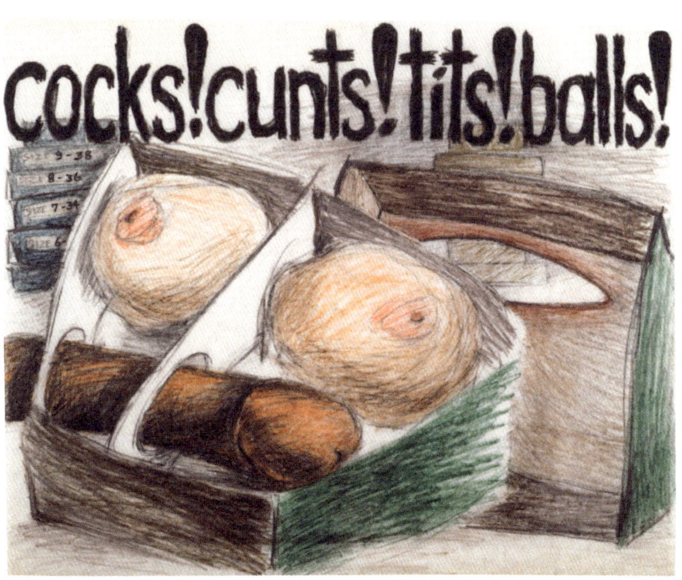

No title, 1962. Crayon on paper, 18½ × 23½ in. (47 × 59.7 cm)

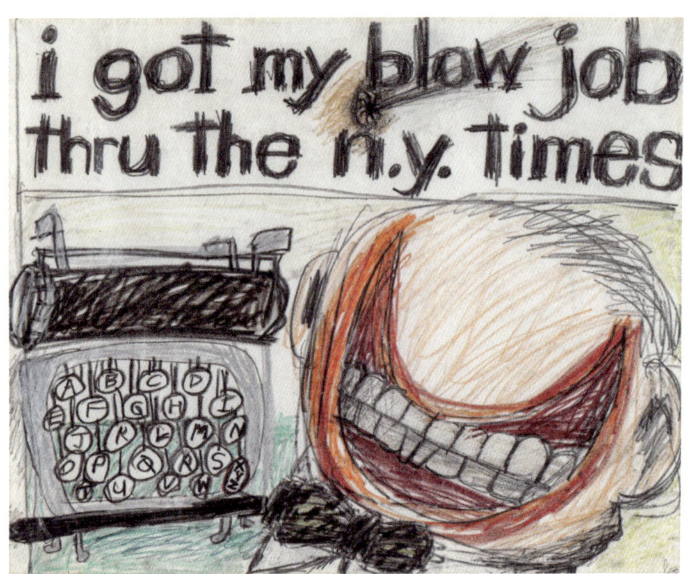

No title, 1962. Crayon on paper, 18¾ × 23⅞ in. (47.6 × 60.6 cm)

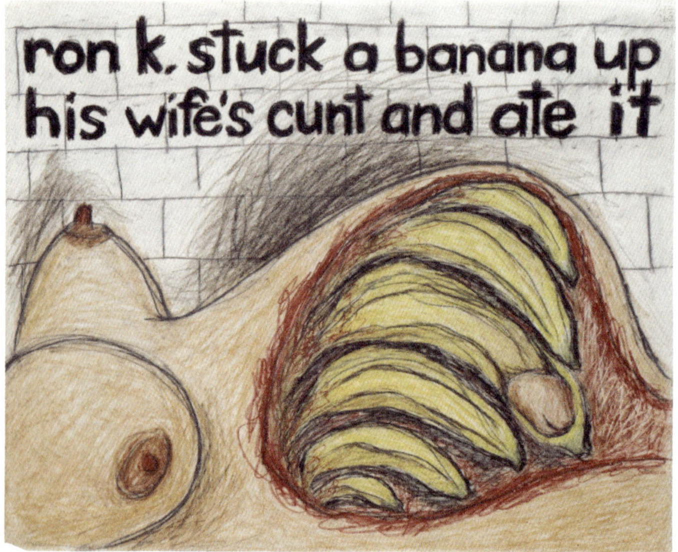

No title, 1962. Colored pencil and crayon on paper, 18¾ × 23⅞ in. (47.6 × 60.5 cm)

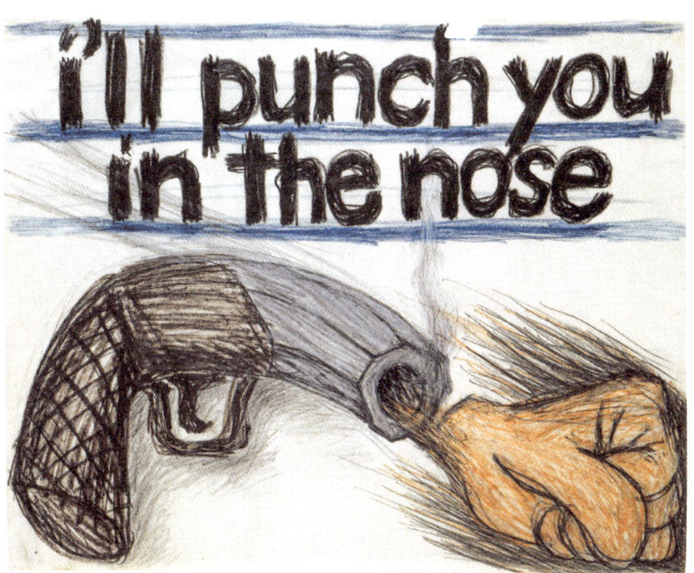

No title, 1962. Colored pencil and crayon on paper, 18¾ × 23⅞ in. (47.6 × 60.5 cm)

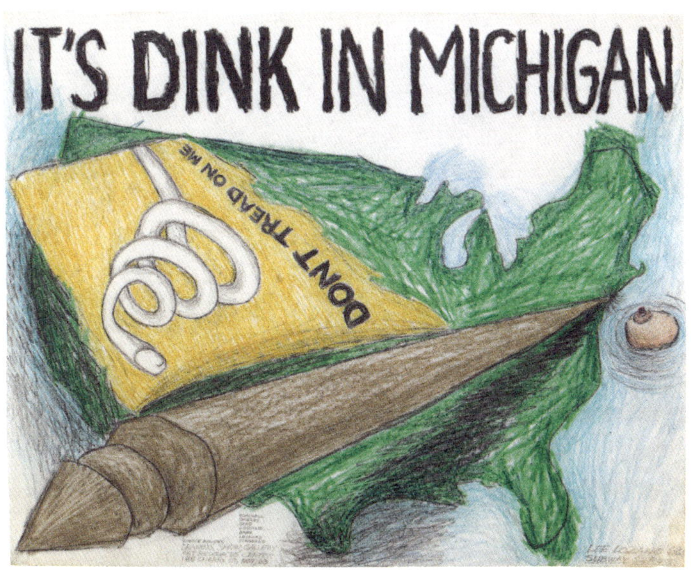

No title, 1962. Crayon and Conté on paper, 18½ × 23½ in. (47 × 59.7 cm)

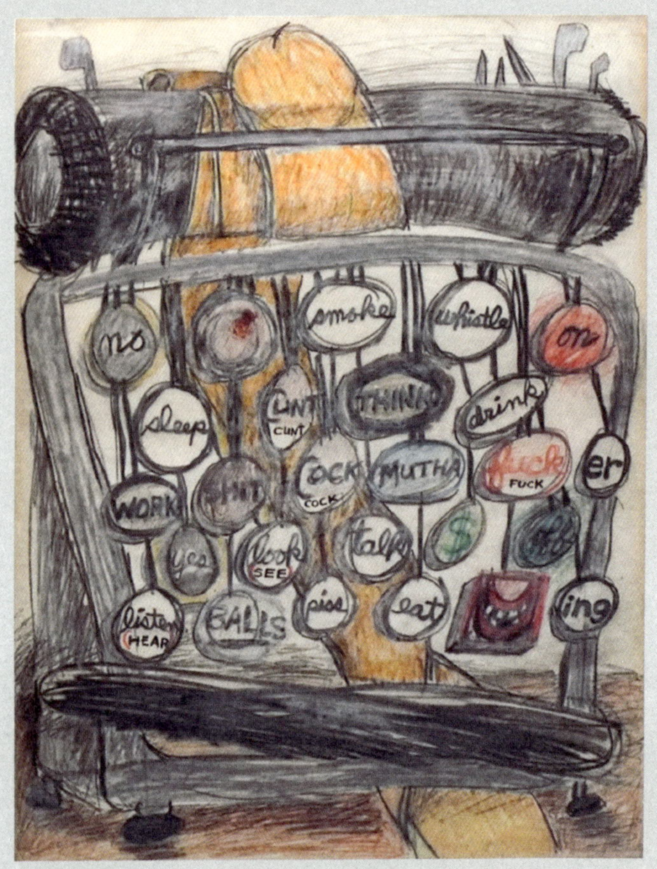

No title, 1962. Graphite and colored pencil on paper, 23¾ × 18¾ in. (60.3 × 47.6 cm)

Lozano and Language

Among the hazardous tools that Lozano mastered, language was one that she wielded devotedly throughout her life. In her early works, scurrilous jokes and curse words are as important as the drawings within her broader project to mock etiquette and disrupt societal expectations. This is encapsulated in one of the works

from her Subway series in which a typewriter is caught
in the process of striking a whole dictionary of things
over a squashed penis, repurposed as paper. The
typewriter is not a neutral symbol: it is both a historically
female-related object, referencing secretarial work,
and the main instrument used by Conceptual artists
at the time to write their "language pieces." "Work,"
"think," "smoke," "sleep,""fuck," "shit," "cunt," "balls,"
"cock," "mutha," and "$" are some of the words placed
on the keys, accompanied by the suffixes "-er" and "-ing,"
in order to transform them into subjects or actions.

The effect of these humorous combinations of words
isn't simply to provoke laughter: for Lozano, puns have
an epistemological value. "Great puns are metaphor in
its purest form," she wrote, suggesting that they allow us
to access deeper strata of reality. Throughout the years,
her puns ranged from trivial gags like "let them eat cock"
(echoing Marie Antoinette's famous motto) to irreverent
yet witty remarks, such as "I will not seek fame, publicity
or suckcess," and contemplative riddles, as in "searching
for a fire with a flashlight." The quasi-philosophical quality
of her puns makes them akin to koans, the paradoxical
questions or statements used in Zen Buddhism to
challenge conventional logical reasoning and encourage
deeper, intuitive insights into reality. Lozano's koans
are "cosmic jokes" in which the Zen precept of listening
to the sound of one hand clapping might have triggered
something closer to a slap. Indeed, in her notebooks she
writes about "Compucianism," a modern religion mixing
Confucianism and puns. Even when she conceived her
ultimate, most dramatic, *Dropout Piece*, she couldn't
resist the temptation to underline its pun value,
noting that you can't spell "dropout" without "pout".

LIST OF TITLES OF PAINTINGS 1964-67 (MAY)
ALL VERBS

REAM
SPIN
VEER
SPAN
CROSS
RAM
PEEL
CHARGE
PITCH
VERGE
SWITCH
SHOOT
SLIDE
CRAM
GOAD
CLASH
CLEAVE
FETCH
CLAMP
LEAN
SWAP
BUTT
CROOK
SPLIT
JUT
HACK
BREACH
STROKE
STOP

No title, 1967. Ink on paper, 11 × 8½ in. (27.9 × 21.6 cm)

Tools and Verbs

In one of the last drawings from her Studio series, dated 1963, a collection of defenseless glandes is displayed as the ultimate trophy of Lozano's castration carnage. The ordered phalli are accompanied by a jubilant announcement: "finally cut them off" (p. 64). From the same year is an iconic photographic portrait of Lozano taken by filmmaker Hollis Frampton. In it, she is leaning on her studio table, gazing directly into the viewer's eyes. Between her and us stands a neatly arrayed set of tools: oversize screws, springs, bolts, bullets, pipes, and carabiners. The symbolic transition from the assortment of cut-out penises to that of hard steel objects seems to convey a warning: I am here, I have weapons, and I am not afraid to use them. Behind her, a wide blank canvas suggests that the size of her paintings was growing, as the tools she depicted became more and more imponent.

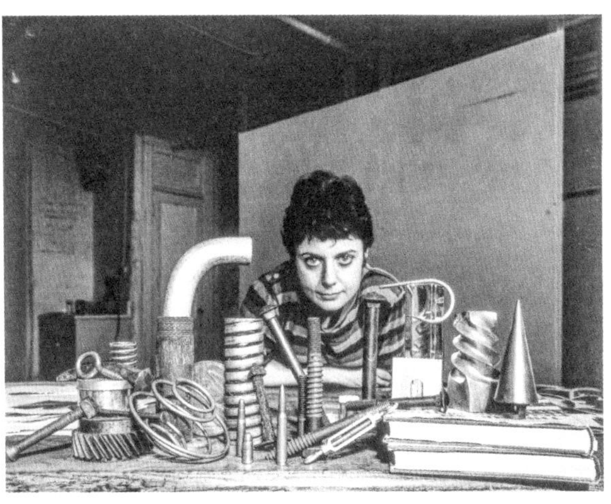

Hollis Frampton, *Lee Lozano*, 1963. Gelatin silver print, 8 × 10 in. (20 × 25 cm)

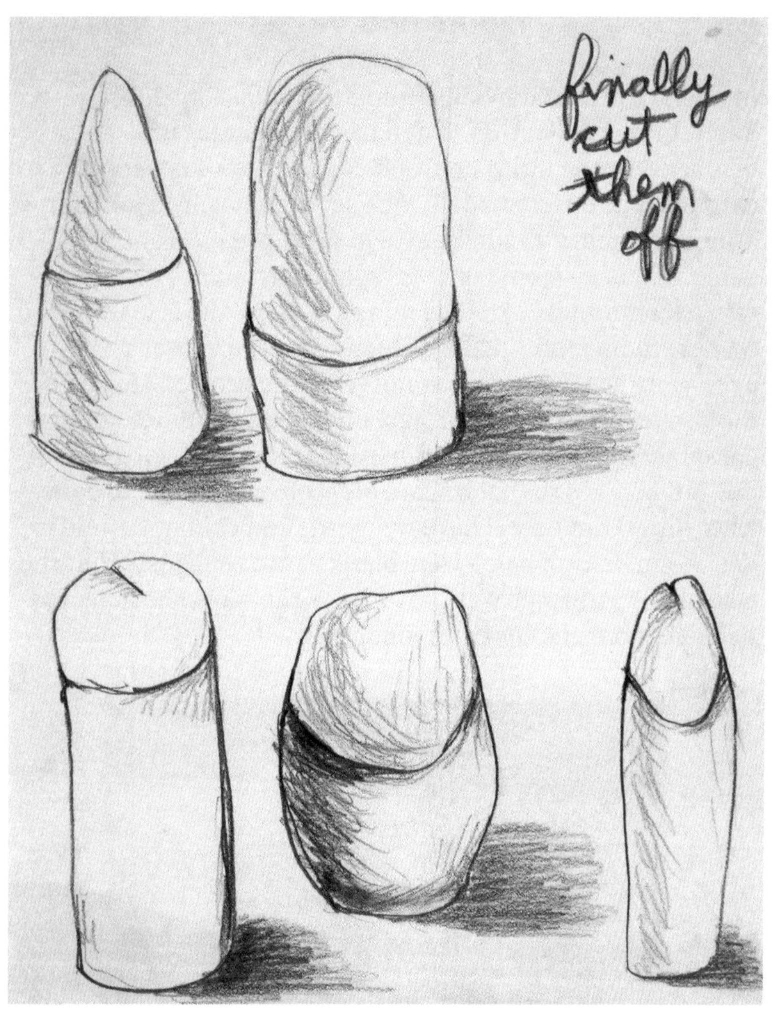

No title, 1963. Graphite on paper, 13¾ × 10¾ in. (35 × 27.4 cm)

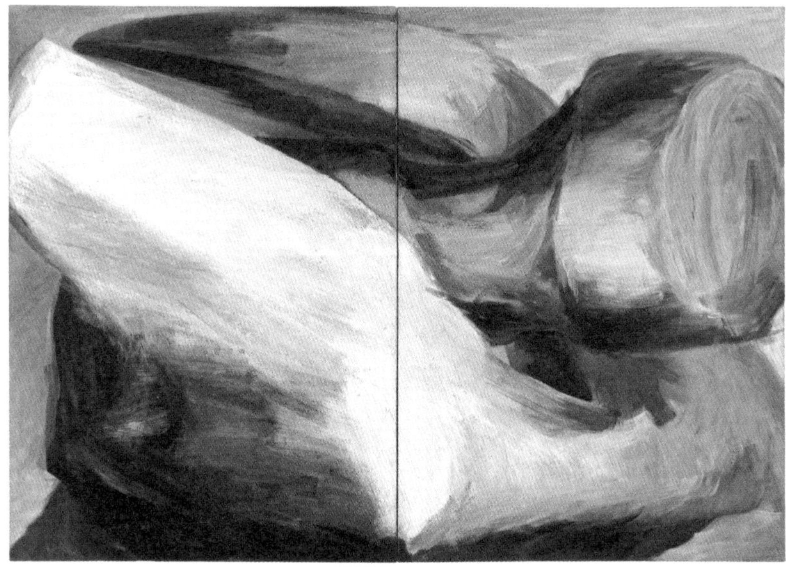

No title, 1963–64. Oil on canvas, two panels, 69 × 100 in. (175.3 × 254 cm)

In the Tools series, the motifs and characters appearing
in the drawings evolve into monumental forms, initially
rendered through bold, expressionistic brushstrokes.
While utensils and instruments dominate the scene,
the human body gradually disappears from Lozano's
visual vocabulary—although traces of anthropomorphic
hints and phallic innuendos persist (pp. 72–75). The metal
items fill the entire canvas, in a double movement that
implies zooming into the object to the point of forcing
it out from the frame's limits. Lozano edges closer to
her subjects, aiming to better capture the energy released
by their movement, carefully observing the behavior
of their material, and exploring their inner structure
at an almost molecular scale. Interest in the symbolic
value of the tools increasingly gives way to a scientific,
almost esoteric engagement with the substance they are

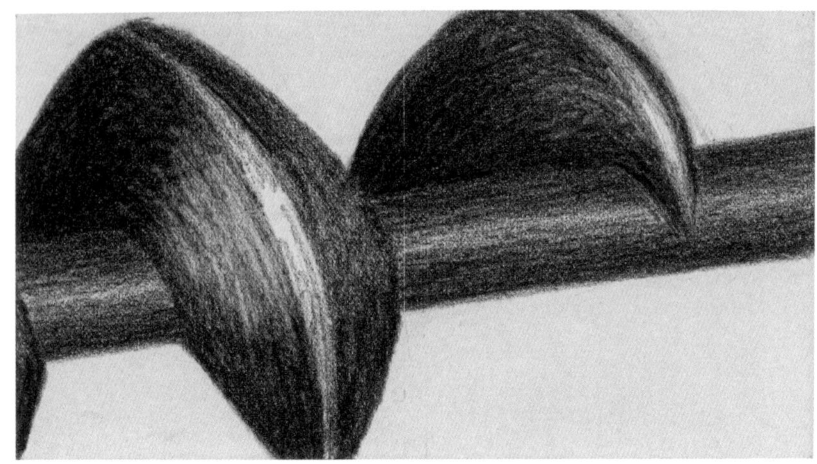

No title, 1964. Graphite on paper, 4⅝ × 8½ in. (11.6 × 21.5 cm)

made of and the force they unleash. Identification with
the inanimate subjects portrayed seems allowed and
encouraged. As she wrote a few years later: "Become a gas,
a charge, a force. Implode to the size of a pea (mass and
weight remain constant, density increases). Turn plastic.
Turn brass and tarnish. Float or fly."

In the attempt to distill the substantial, rather than
the expressionistic, quality of her subjects, Lozano's
strokes became less dense and increasingly thinner,
ordered, and precise. Her paintings started to flirt with
the language of Minimalism, with wide stretches of color
meticulously arranged on the canvas (pp. 76–79). Her
practice adopted traits drawn from the hard sciences:
compositions were built with mathematical precision and
colors juxtaposed according to Gestalt principles. She
began reading more of *Scientific American* and *Physics Today*
and having in-depth conversations with her neighbor
Ed Feldman, a mathematician, who introduced her to

René Thom's "catastrophe theory"—the idea that there exists an underlying mathematical system responsible for stability as well as sudden disruptions in dynamic systems. The scientification of her thinking was irreversible: "if I were an old-fashioned man I would say that art was my wife, but science (physics) was my mistress," Lozano stated in 1968. "Science is on my mind all the time & when I think about it I get hot pants."

Around 1964 it became clear that the reference to one or more specific objects had grown to be superfluous for her work: she started aiming at directly representing the forces and energies underpinning the superficial, object-based strata of our reality. *Ream*, *Pin*, *Veer*, *Span*, *Cross*, *Ram*, *Peel*, *Charge*, *Pitch*, *Verge*, *Switch*, *Shoot*, *Slide*, *Cram*, *Goad*, *Clash*, *Cleave*, *Fetch*, *Clamp*, *Lean*, *Swap*, *Butt*, *Crook*, *Split*, *Jut*, *Hack*, *Breach*, *Stroke*, and *Stop* are the titles of her works from 1964 to 1967. In a write-up dated May 1967, Lozano lists them one below the other as verses of a poem, or as the summary of an experimental protocol (p. 62). The document acted also as a chronological reminder, used to claim the originality of her work among (against) her peers. Indeed, her write-up came right after the publication of Richard Serra's *Verb List* (1967; p. 68), a similar description of activities he usually performed in the studio, such as "to cut, to flow, to lift, to modulate, to bind, to hook." Lozano's last title, *Stop*, seems like a not-too-subtle rebuke to Serra's last verb: "to continue."

While Serra's sculptural practice incorporated industrial processes and metalworking methods, Lozano's studio was morphing into a physics lab. "Everything 'important' I seem to have discovered exactly as a scientist uses the method of observation and experimentation," she later stated. In 1967 she even started making preparatory sketches for her paintings in large notebooks meant for students of scientific disciplines. They document Lozano's process until 1970, ending with the production of the *Wave* series, in which the combination of art, science, and existence reaches its critical point.

Richard Serra, *Verb List*, 1967. Graphite on paper, two sheets, each 10 × 8½ in. (25.4 × 21.6 cm)

In Pictures

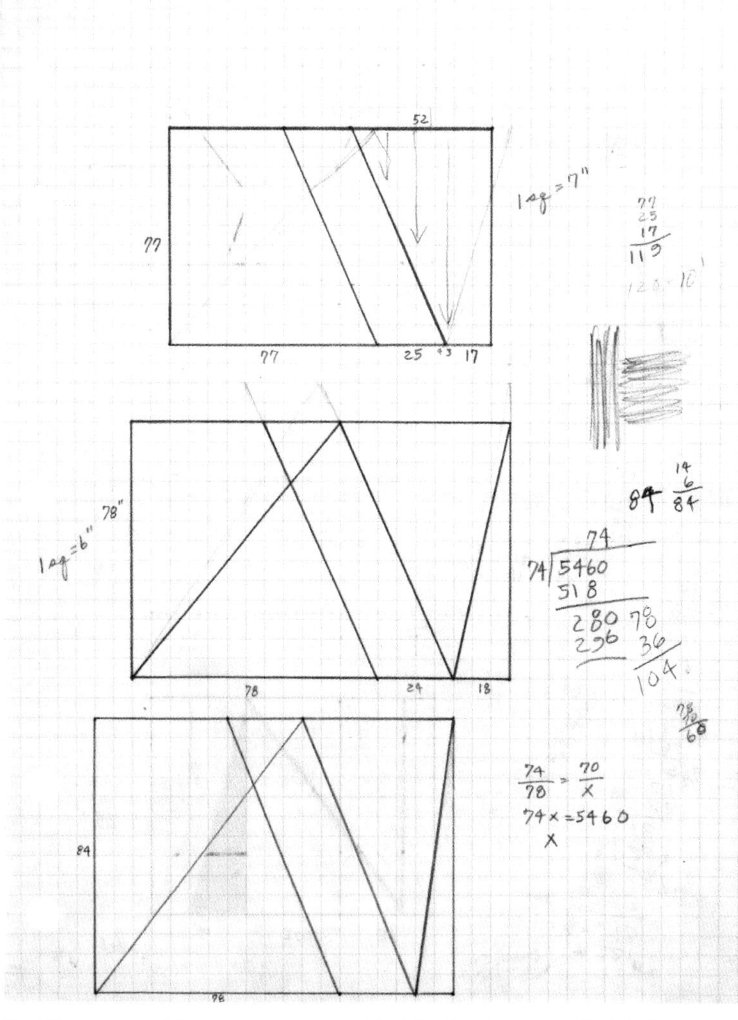

No title, n.d. Graphite on graph paper, 10½ × 8 in. (26.8 × 20.2 cm). This drawing is a study for the painting *Lean* (1966; pp. 76–77)

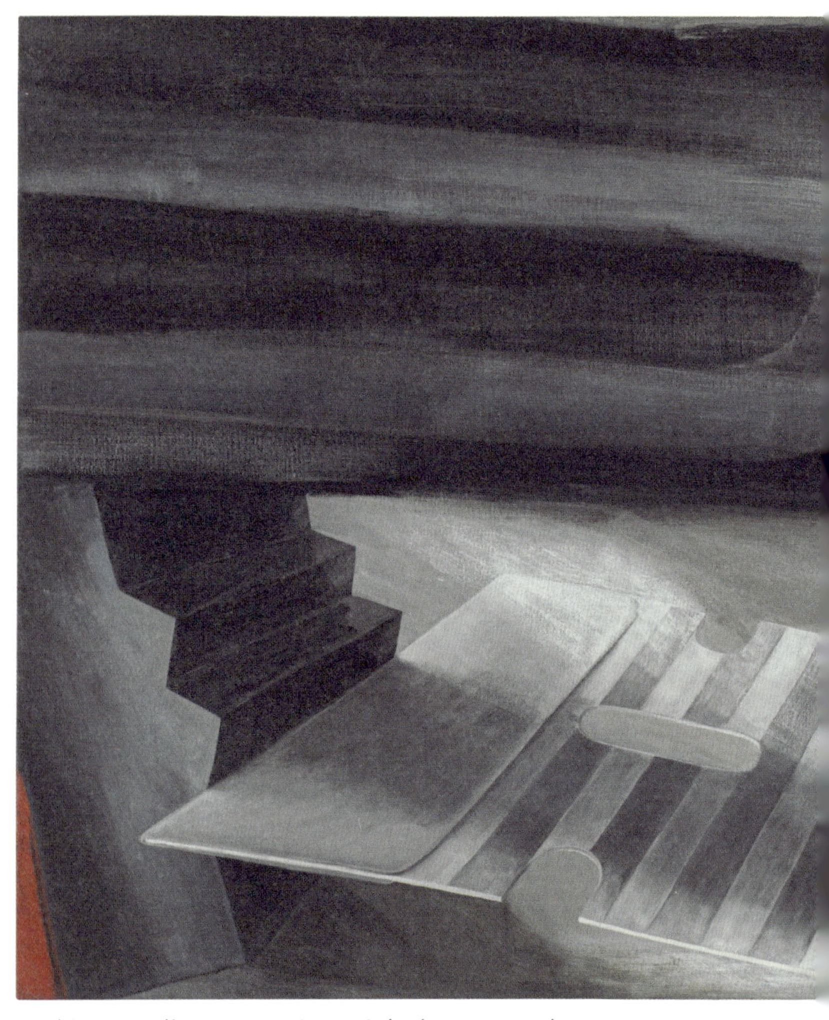

No title, 1964. Oil on canvas, 65¾ × 118¾ in. (167 × 301.5 cm)

In Pictures

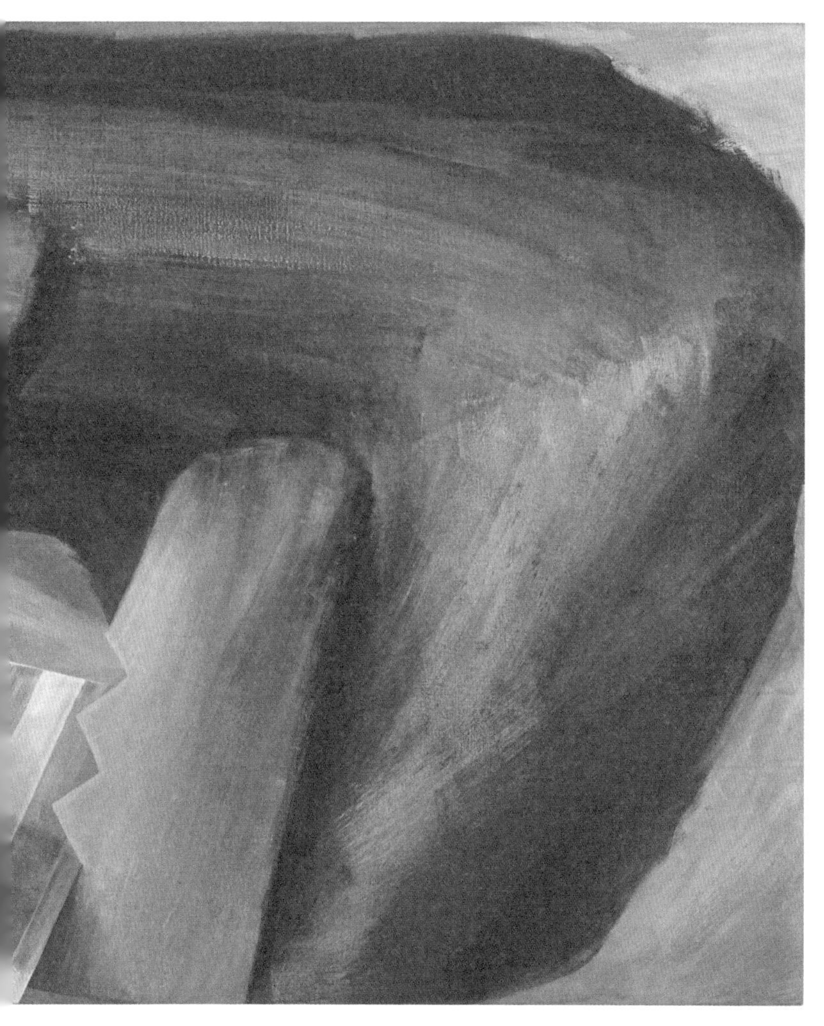

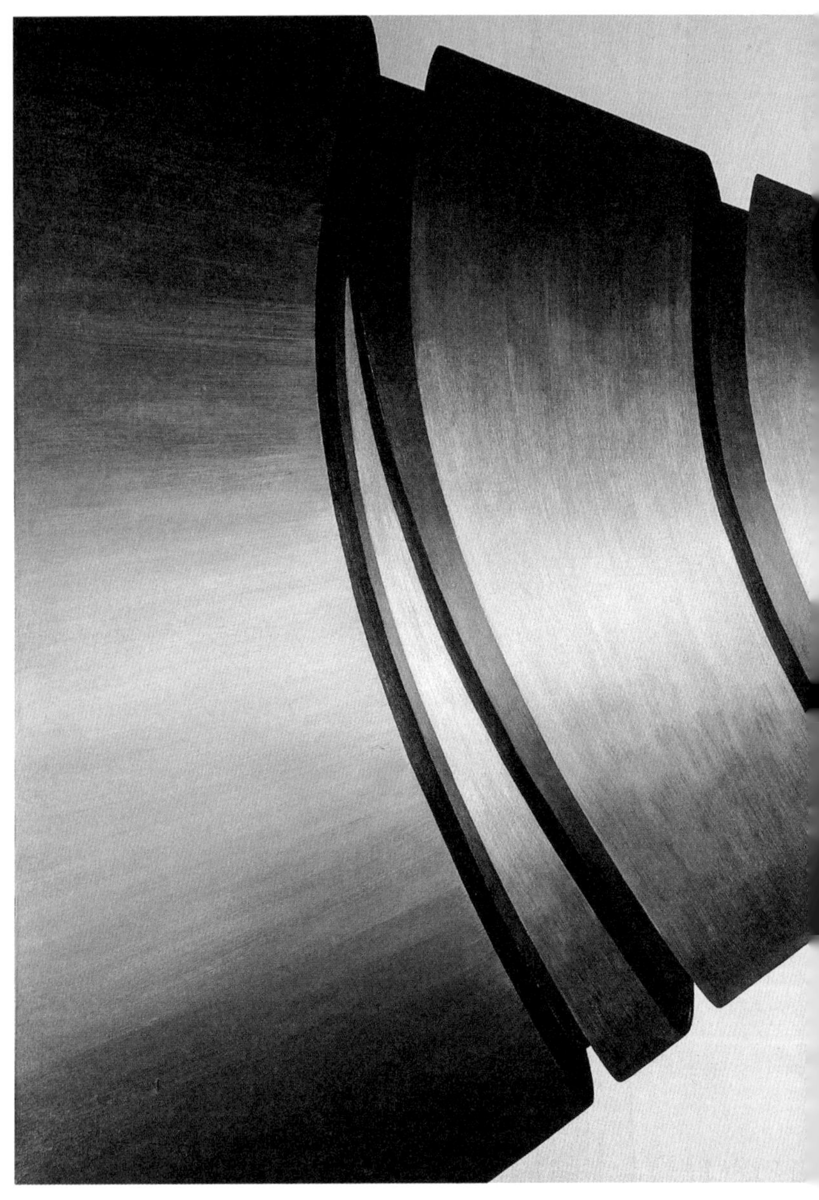

Ream, 1964. Oil on canvas, 78 × 96 in. (198.1 × 243.8 cm)

In Pictures

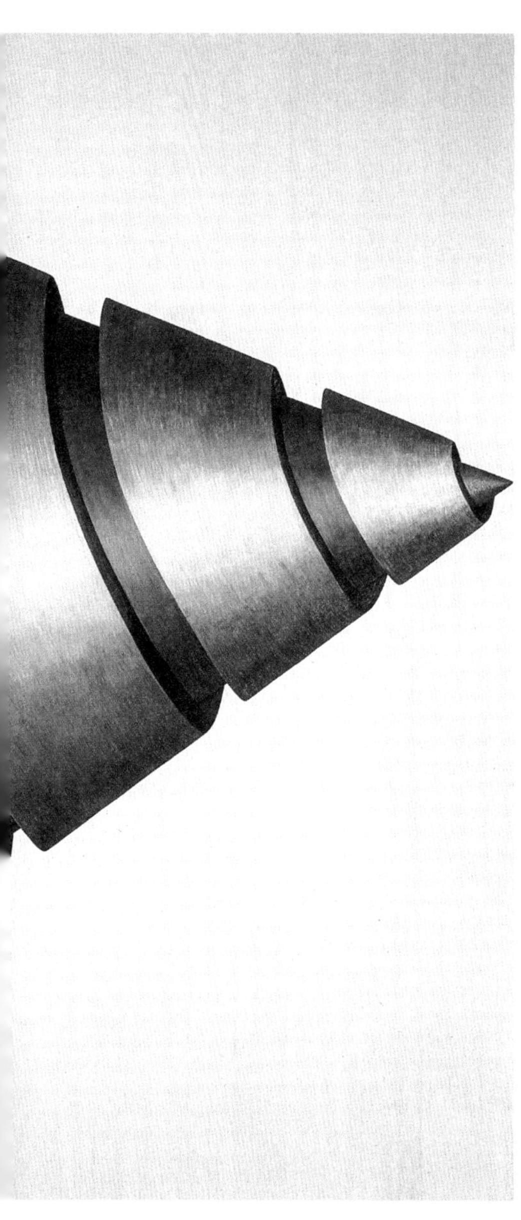

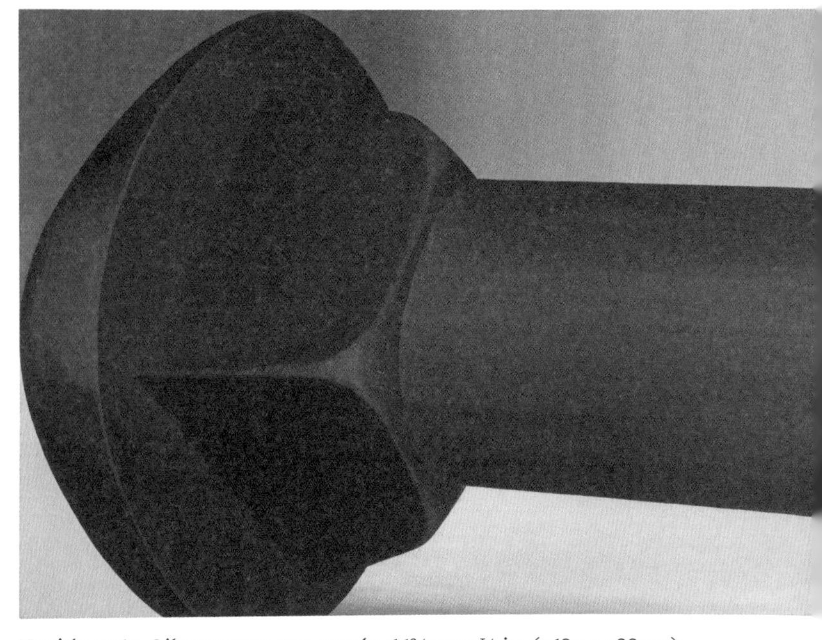

No title, 1964. Oil on canvas, two panels, 66⅜ × 192⅛ in. (168.5 × 488 cm)

In Pictures

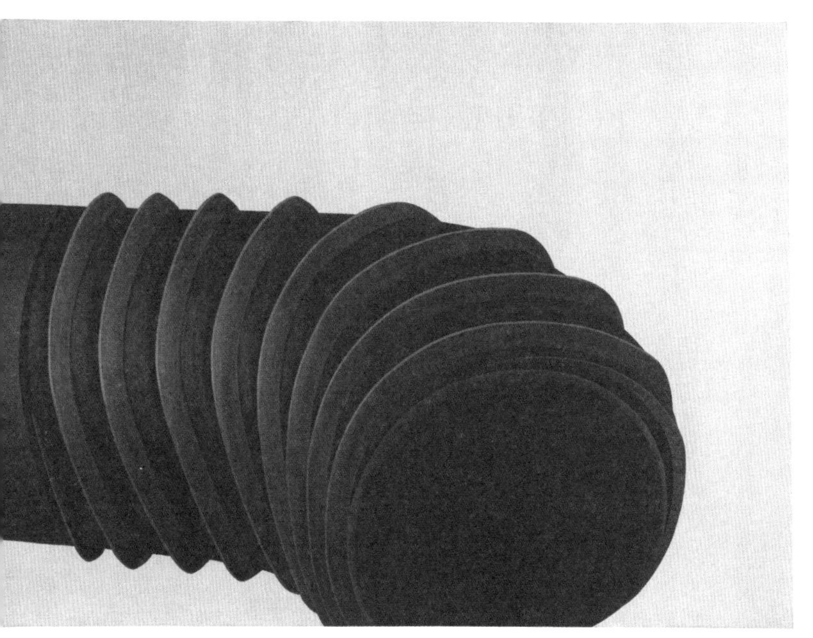

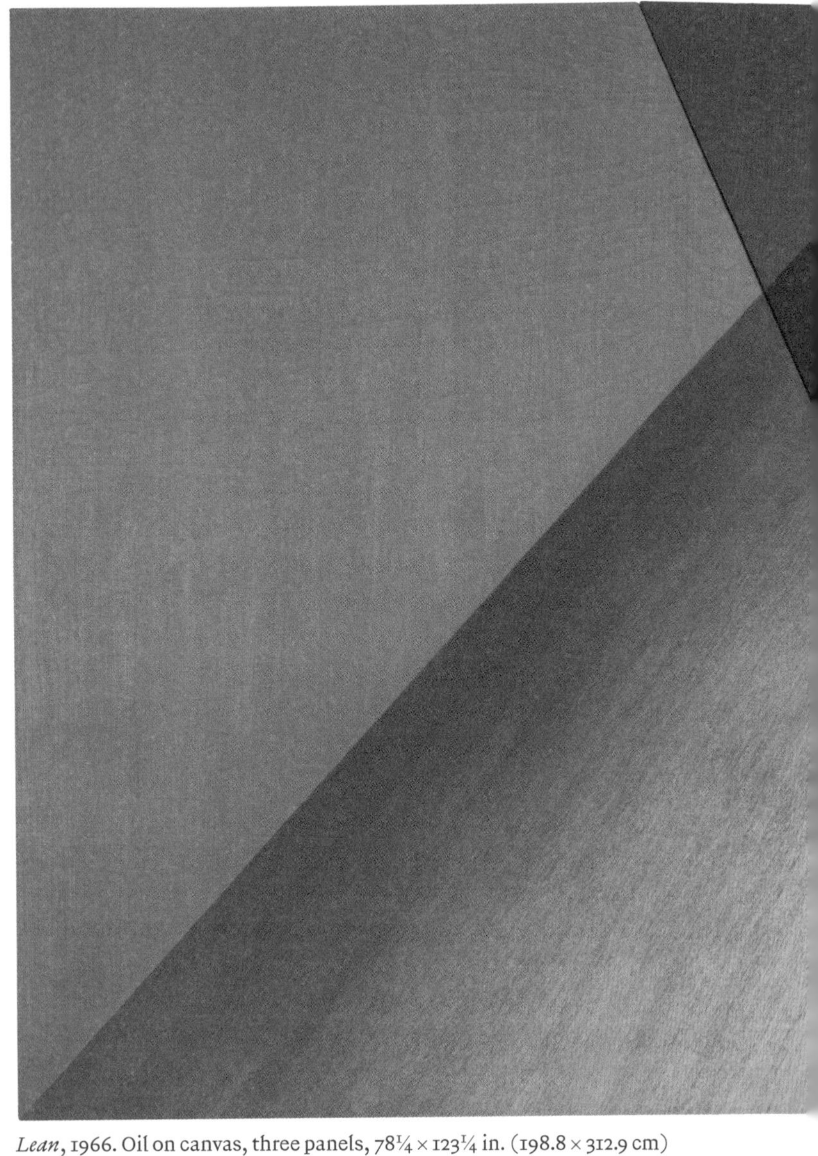

Lean, 1966. Oil on canvas, three panels, 78¼ × 123¼ in. (198.8 × 312.9 cm)

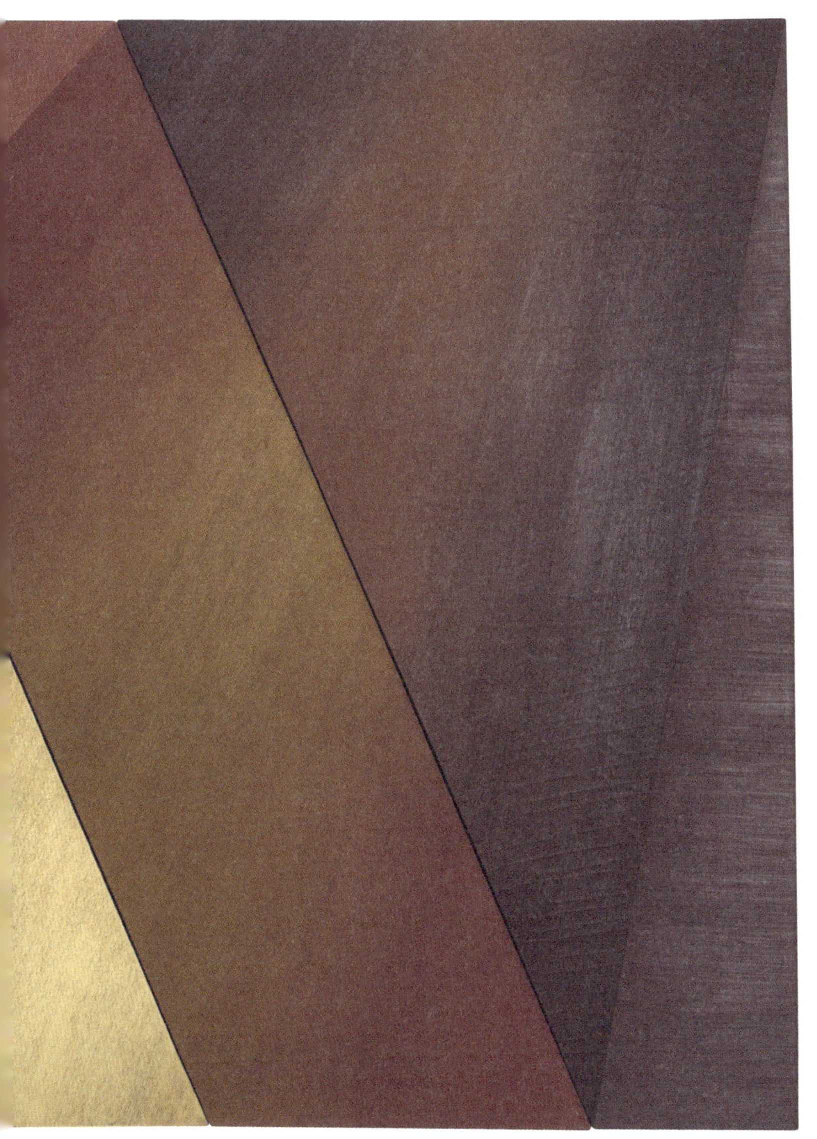

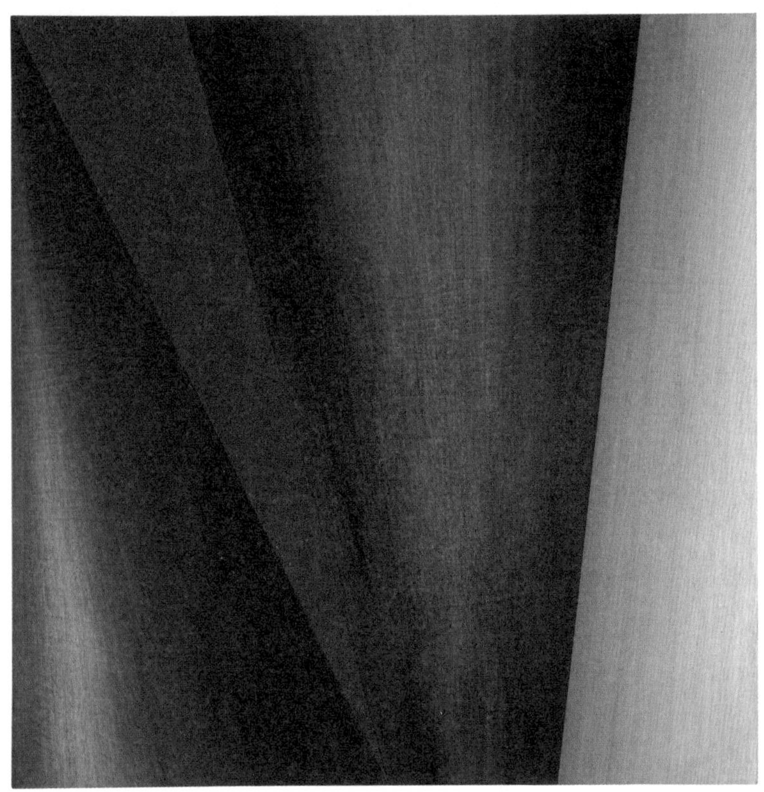

Cram, 1965. Oil on canvas, 78 × 78 in. (198.1 × 198.1 cm)

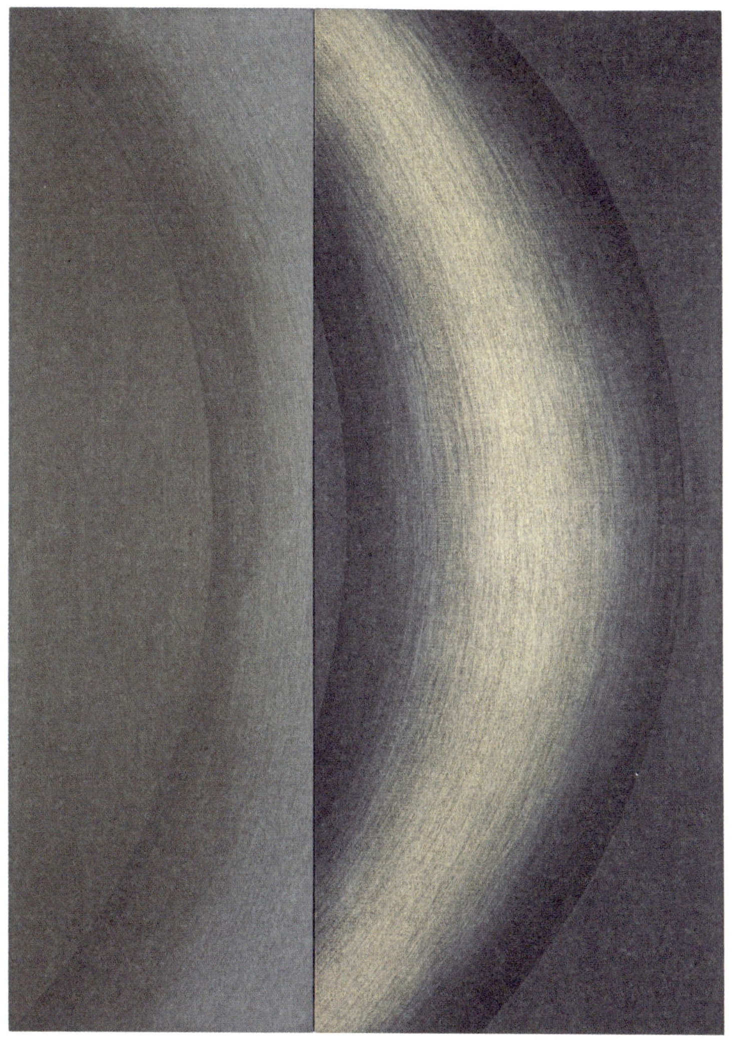

Crook, 1968. Oil on canvas, two panels, 96¼ × 70 in. (244.4 × 177.8 cm)

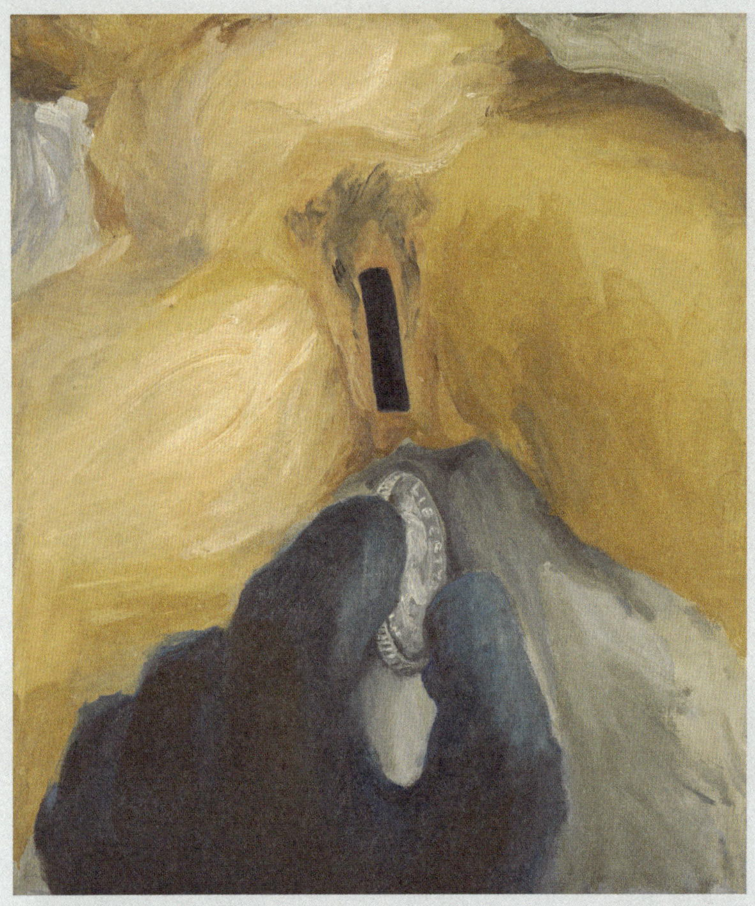

No title, 1962. Oil on canvas, 33 × 29 in. (83.8 × 73.7 cm)

Keep the Machine Well Greased

Before shifting nearly exclusively to the representation
of gigantic tools, Lozano focused on creating a raw,
visceral catalog of human and mechanical subjects,
often entangled with one another. Her paintings built
upon the legacy of a modernist trope—the relationship

between the human body and the machine—but morphed it into grotesque representations filled with dark humor. In some of the canvases, Lozano's "body = machine" imagery almost verges on dystopian science fiction. In a painting from 1962, a female body, posed in a way that echoes Gustave Courbet's *L'Origine du monde* (1866), is ruthlessly transformed into a vending machine. Between the spread thighs, a black geometric mark replaces the vagina, revealing that the opening is, in fact, a coin slot. The scene is constructed as a POV shot: in the foreground, a hand wearing a blue glove is about to insert a quarter into the opening. The word "Liberty" engraved on the coin captions the uncanny transaction with a classic Lozano pun.

The replacement of the human body with a more efficient mechanical system was a recurring preoccupation. In 1968, Lozano noted that, "Whoever or whatever designed human beings & all evolutionary forms that led up to them was a bad artist who took the idea of form follows function to its ultimate disaster." She suggested redesigning the human being, replacing its face with a control panel indicating changing states of temperature, metabolism, adrenaline levels, brain sodium/potassium balance, and other bodily functions. "Let the eyes be redesigned to look inward as well as out," she continued, asking why we are denied information about the inside of our bodies. Her work could be seen, to a certain extent, as a visionary answer to the lack she was seeing in the "elaborate container" that is our body. This is most evident in her Airplane series, where the flying objects she portrays are finally allowed to enter orifices and holes, artist emissaries on an adventure of discovery through human flesh.

Private Books

Between 1968 and 1970, Lozano kept a series of eleven pocket-sized notebooks, each numbered and labeled "private" on the cover. These notebooks contain both intimate and mundane details about her daily life; defiant, manifesto-like statements about art and politics; ideas for paintings; pithy aphorisms; and pronouncements, often caustic, about the art world and her peers. While several of the "Life-Art" pieces first recorded in these notebooks were later rerecorded and presented as formal artworks, many—including *Dropout Piece*— are only documented in these pages.

The four notebook entries included here, dated between April 1968 and September 1969, are longer statements that reveal Lozano's mounting frustration with the art world and its social order, offering different proposals for resistance. (In seeking to preserve Lozano's voice, the transcriptions of her writings reproduce the spacing, punctuation, and spelling of the originals as faithfully as possible.)

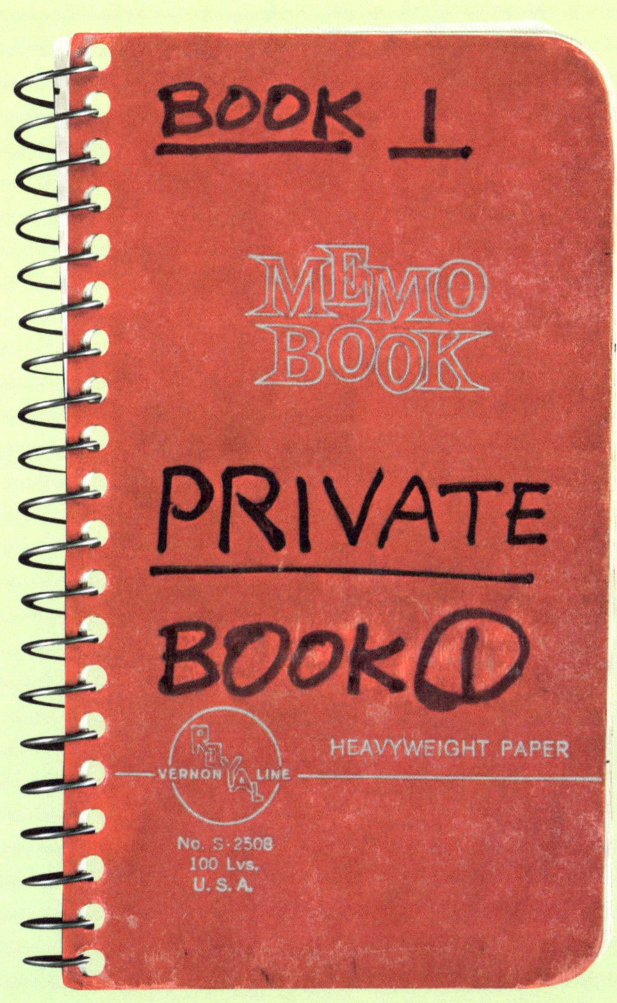

BOOK 1
MEMO BOOK
PRIVATE
BOOK ①
HEAVYWEIGHT PAPER
ROYAL
VERNON LINE
No. S-2508
100 Lvs.
U.S.A.

I COULD START WRITING DOWN <u>ALL</u> MY FANTASIES.

I COULD RECORD * NUMBER OF INCOMING CALLS
REC'D EACH DAY, FROM WHOM, CONTENT OF EACH,
ALSO CALLS OUTGOING.

<u>REAL JUNKIE PLAY</u>

* BY COINCIDENCE I ACTUALLY START THIS ALMOST
EXACTLY A YEAR LATER

HAVE A SHOW OF PAINTINGS HUNG ON BRILLIANT
WHITE WALLS IN A BRILLIANTLY LIT GALLERY.
SPECIAL LIGHTS OR SLIDES FROM ABOVE
(AND OPPOSITE) WILL CAST A DEEP SHADOW
OVER PAINTING (NOT SPILLING OVER ONTO WALLS).
THIS DEVICE (1) SAVES ARTIST EMBAREASSMENT
OF HAVING WORK <u>SEEN</u> BY PEOPLE WHO THEN
FEEL THEY HAVE TO SAY SOMETHING ABOUT IT (2)
ENHANCES MYSTERY OF PNTINGS (3) SAVES TROUBLE
OF HAVING TO LIGHT PNTINGS "CORRECTLY." (4) GIVES
HINT OF "EXCITING COLOR" (VOMIT) BUT FORCES
OBSERVER TO SEE MORE IMPORTANT THINGS ABOUT
CANVAS THAN COLOR, SUCH AS FORM, DIRECTIONAL
APPLICATION OF PNT, TEXTURE, AND MAYBE
<u>ENERGY</u> DISEMBODIED FROM <u>ANY</u> EMOTIONAL
COLOR ASSOCIATIONS, EVEN THOSE WITH WHITE,
GRAY AND BLK.

HOW CAN I MAKE ENERGY PNTINGS (LIKE E.G. BALL-
AND LINE-PNTINGS, WHICH MOVE IN THE OBSERVER'S

MIND) <u>ALL</u> <u>PAINT-</u> <u>AND</u> <u>ENERGY-PNTINGS</u> <u>SANS</u> COLOR,
EVEN SANS BLK-GRAY-WH?

TRY AN OLD IDEA OF MINE. MIX TWO OR MORE
STRONGLY CONTRASTING COLORS ON BRUSH, APPLY
TO CANVAS WITH CONSISTENT BUT ROUGH STREAKED-
MIX PROCESS (MAYBE "PROCESS" JUST MEANS
<u>TECHNIQUE</u>, THAT FILTHY WORD) WHICH CAN ONLY
BE SEEN, NOT DESCRIBED VERBALLY. [FIRST FUCK UP
THE PHOTOGRAPHERS, THEN THE PRINTERS, THEN
THE CRITICS, AND <u>ALWAYS</u> THE ARCHITECTS]. THE
SENSTATION OF <u>SPEED</u>, BLURRED COLORS MOVING
FAST AND / OR WITH GREAT ENERGY, OUGHT TO
TRANSCEND ANY <u>PARTICULAR</u> COLOR SENSATION
OR ASSOCIATION.

PERHAPS THIS IDEA OUGHT TO BE TRIED IN WAVE
SERIES.*

NO, BUT MAYBE IT'S GOOD FOR <u>STONED</u>, <u>DRUNK</u>,
<u>SOBER</u>.

<u>SEPT 25, 68</u>

BOYCOTT GALLERIES & DEALERS TOO. COLLECTORS
CHOSEN BY ARTIST AS "ALLOWED TO BUY" STRICTLY
ON BASIS OF HOW INTERESTING THEY ARE WHEN THEY
VISIT ARTIST. COLLECTORS AS ENTERTAINMENT FOR
ARTISTS. PRICE OF ART FIXED, PLUS EXACT COST OF
MATERIALS AND / OR TRANSPORTATION, EACH ARTIST
DECIDES ONE PRICE THAT IS SAME FOR EACH WORK
REGARDLESS OF SIZE OR LOCATION: "I AM A $1000
ARTIST," "I AM A $200 ARTIST," "I AM A $10,000."

<u>SEPT 25, CONT.</u>

COLLECTORS WOULD BE RATED ON BASIS OF POPULARITY WITH ARTISTS. "I AM A 50-ARTIST COLLECTOR, 50 ARTISTS HAVE LIKED ME ENOUGH TO LET ME PAY FOR THEIR WORK," "I AM A 7-ARTIST COLLECTOR," "I AM A 1,328-ARTIST COLLECTOR." CONVERSATION AT THE BAR: "COLLECTOR S. IS THE MOST POPULAR, THE MOST ARTISTS HAVE LET HIM PAY." "YES, BUT LOOK AT WHO THE ARTISTS ARE, THEY ARE JERKS, THEY WOULD LIKE ANYBODY."

<u>MAY 19 [1969]</u>

IN THINKING ABT HOW THE WORK OF ARTISTS I HAVE KNOWN FOR A WHILE ([ROBERT] MORRIS & [YVONNE] RAINER PERFECT EXAMPLES OF THIS) GIVES LESS & LESS FEEDBACK TO ME EACH YEAR UNTIL FINALLY THIS YEAR I DIDN'T WANT TO EXPERIENCE IT ANY MORE (PART OF <u>GENERAL STRIKE</u> WAS "TO NOT GO ANYMORE"), ALTHOUGH I CONSIDER THESE PEOPLE IMPORTANT ARTISTS (IN FACT OLD MASTERS), I REALIZE THE FOLLOWING:

THE <u>DIALOGUE PIECE</u> COMES THE CLOSEST SO FAR TO AN IDEAL I HAVE OF A KIND OF ART THAT WOULD NEVER CEASE RETURNING FEEDBACK TO ME OR TO OTHERS, WHICH CONTINUALLY REFRESHES ITSELF WITH NEW INFORMATION, WHICH APPROACHES AN IDEAL MERGER OF FORM AND CONTENT, WHICH CAN NEVER BE "FINISHED", WHICH CAN NEVER RUN OUT OF MATERIAL, WHICH DOESN'T INVOLVE "THE ARTIST & THE OBSERVER" BUT MAKES BOTH PARTICIPANTS

ARTIST & OBSERVER SIMULTANEOUSLY, WHICH IS
NOT FOR SALE, WHICH IS DEMOCRATIC, WHICH IS NOT
DIFFICULT TO MAKE, WHICH IS INEXPENSIVE TO MAKE,
WHICH CAN NEVER BE COMPLETELY UNDERSTOOD,
PARTS OF WHICH WILL ALWAYS REMAIN MYSTERIOUS &
UNKNOWN, WHICH IS UNPREDICTABLE & PREDICTABLE
AT THE SAME TIME, IN FACT, THIS PIECE APPROACHES
HAVING EVERYTHING I ENJOY OR SEEK ABT ART, AND
IT CANNOT BE PUT IN A GALLERY, ALTHOUGH SOME
ASPECTS OF IT COULD BE "EXHIBITED" IF SO DESIRED.

SOONER OR LATER IF THE DIALOGUE PIECE REMAINS
PERPETUALLY IN PROCESS I'LL INVITE EVERYBODY
FOR A DIALOGUE.

WHAT IF I STOPPED DOING DIFFERENT PIECES & JUST
DID THE DIALOGUE PIECE FOR THE REST OF MY LIFE
AS MY "WORK"? I COULD MOVE TO AN EXOTIC PLACE
& DO IT THERE; IT HAS NO SPACE OR TIME BOUNDRIES.

I WILL INVITE EACH PERSON ONLY ONCE SO THAT
NOBODY GETS BORED (ALTHOUGH ANYONE IS
WELCOME TO COME BACK).

SOME PEOPLE WILL REFUSE TO COME OR NEVER
SHOW UP. THIS MAKES THE PIECE "CHALLENGING."

AFTER A WHILE I COULD START INVITING STRANGERS
FOR A DIALOGUE, WHICH WOULD MAKE IT "SURPRISING."

I DON'T KNOW WHETHER THE DIALOGUE PIECE WILL
FULFILL THE IDEA OF AN IDEAL PIECE, BUT AS I SAID,
SO FAR IT SEEMS TO COME CLOSEST TO THIS IN
ITS POTENTIAL.

AFTER SEEING ARTICLE IN <u>LIFE</u> RE $ ART I AM MORE
SURE THAN EVER THAT I WISH TO DO <u>PIECES</u> THAT
HAVE SUBJECT MATTER ONLY HIGHLY RELEVANT
TO MY LIFE, THAT CAN FEED BACK INFO NECESSARY
TO MY PERSONAL SURVIVAL, THAT IS UNPREDICTABLE
IN IN ITS FEEDBACK & FROM WHICH I CAN "LEARN,"
OR WHICH IS DANGEROUS, OR WHICH "DOCUMENTS"
ACTS (ART-LIKE) STARTED LONG AGO. I AM
INTERESTED IN OPEN-ENDED INVESTIGATIONS,
NOT CLOSED-CIRCLE (EFFETE) STATEMENTS
ABOUT FORM (MANIPULATION).
<u>SELF-SURVIVAL</u> ART.

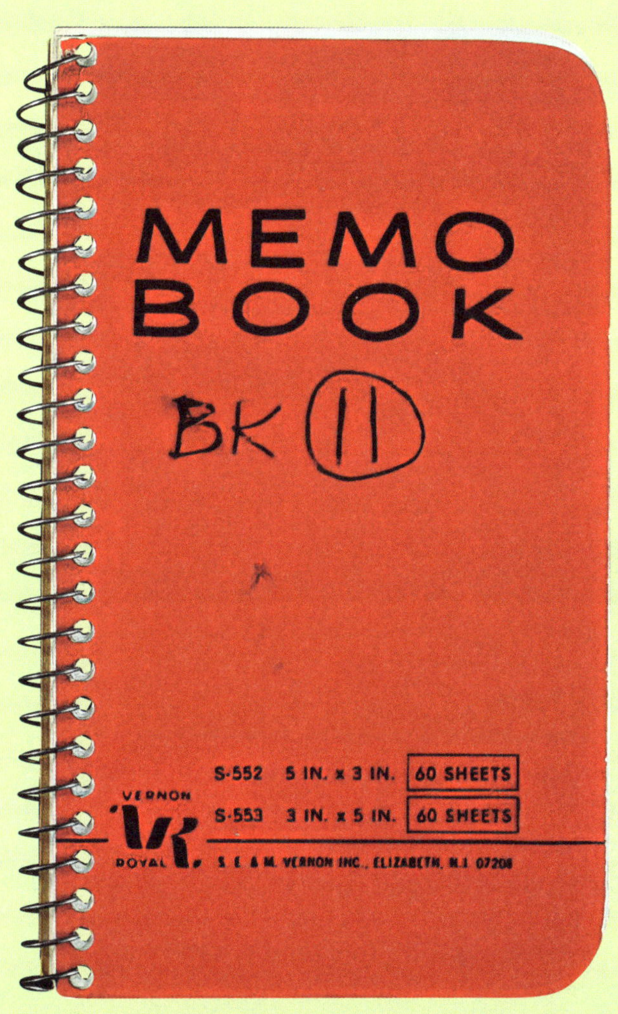

MEMO
BOOK
BK 11
S-552   5 IN. x 3 IN.   60 SHEETS
S-553   3 IN. x 5 IN.   60 SHEETS
VERNON
'VR
ROYAL, S. E. & M. VERNON INC., ELIZABETH, N.J. 07208

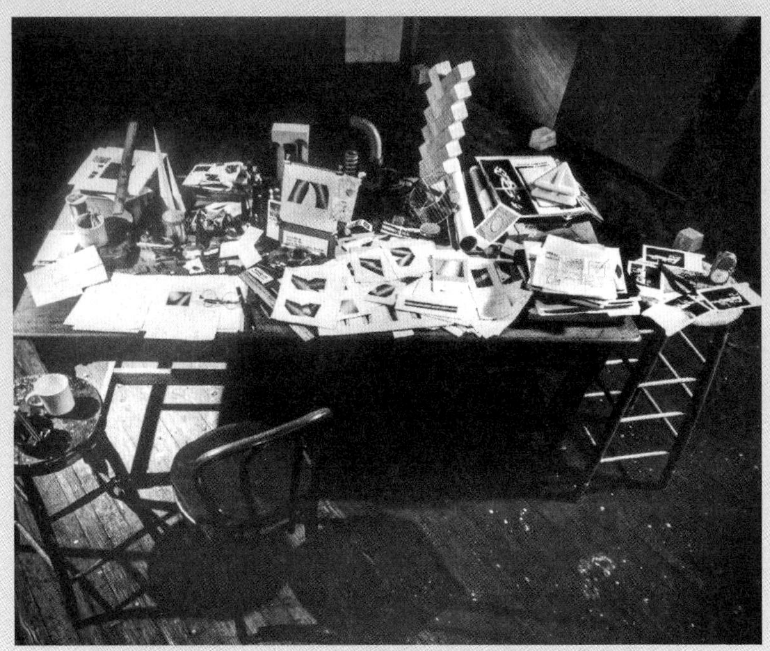

Hollis Frampton's photograph of Lozano's table, 1966

Lozano's Table

Another photograph by Hollis Frampton, from 1966, seems to encapsulate the shift in Lozano's work and self-representation. The center of the set is, again, Lozano's worktable—yet, while in 1963 it served mainly as a base for the tools, and as a stage for the artist's fierce presence (p. 63), this time it is the main subject of the photograph. Shot from above, it displays a messy composition of preparatory drawings and writings, clippings from magazines, invitations, and direct references to other artists, including a small sculpture, *Cock* (1963), by Carl Andre. Some of the tools displayed in the first image are still visible, partially obscured by all the objects that have accumulated since. The body of the artist is absent, yet Lozano's eyeglasses, coffee cup, and cigarettes are still there, as if she just left the chair. It is noteworthy that the photograph was chosen by Lozano for the invitation to her first solo exhibition at Bianchini Gallery. The image communicates how the object of attention is slowly shifting from work to process, from the artist to the environment that surrounds her.

More than a random accumulation of ephemera, this gargantuan pile held importance for Lozano, who would eventually deem it her *Table Piece* ("one of the biggest & oldest <u>pieces</u>"). Started in 1962, the work ended abruptly in January 1972, when Lozano had to leave her studio and the "geological strata" of her table had to go, along with everything else. The table also had a historiographical purpose, hosting printed matter relating to the art scene. One of her first "Life-Art" pieces states: "When you're 'trying to make it' keep going for years a pile of show announcements, press release material, all printed matter relating to the art scene. Everything that comes in the mail or is accumulated other ways is tossed on the pile. When you 'start to make it' throw your own printed matter on the pile. Let it be covered up by time the way everybody else's is." This severe encouragement to scale down one's hubris was followed by a more conciliatory possibility, to be followed in the event of a self-esteem emergency: "<u>Companion piece</u>: Toss your own printed matter on top of the pile and keep it on top of the pile" (p. 38).

WHITNEY MUSEUM OF AMERICAN ART

945 Madison Avenue at Seventy-Fifth Street   New York, New York 10021   (212) 249-4100

For Release WITHOUT THE ARTIST'S INSPECTION
11-20-70
On receipt

A special exhibition [?] of eleven ~~"sound wave" panel~~ WAVE SERIES paintings by the New York artist, Lee Lozano, will open at the Whitney Museum on December 2 and continue through January 3, 1971. The works will be installed in the Lobby Gallery.

The ~~image,~~ METAPHOR upon which ~~Miss Lozano's~~ THE IMAGE OF THE paintings ~~are~~ IS based, is that of ~~the sinuous pattern of sound waves as recorded visually by electronic devices.~~ EXTENDED ELECTROMAGNETIC SPECTRUM; THE SIZE OF EACH PANEL, 96" x 42" (ANY OF THE 4 WAYS IS UP); ~~The size of wavelengths, even factors of 96 (except last panel); the medium, oilpaint; the principle, repetitive curves of pulsating sound became a theme, which the artist explores in variations.~~ THE SIZE OF WAVELENGTHS, EVEN FACTORS OF 96 (EXCEPT LAST PANEL); THE MEDIUM, OILPAINT; THE PRINCIPLE, WHAT HAPPENS WHEN WAVES OF PAINT GET SHORTER & SHALLOWER; THE METHOD, USE SAME BRUSH FOR EACH WAVELENGTH & PAINT EACH WAVEAREA IN ONE SESSION; THE BRUSH, 3" WIDTH HOUSEPAINT BRISTLE (MELLOW); ~~The pattern of the image is enhanced by the finely wrought texture of the painted surface.~~ THE RESULTS, LENGTH OF WAVEPAINTING SESSION INVERSELY PROPORTIONAL TO LENGTH OF WAVE, METHOD STRINGENCY CAUSE OF ELIMINATION OF 2ND COLOR AFTER FIRST SIX PANELS, PATCHINESS OF PAINT IN SHORTER WAVELENGTHS; STATE OF ARTIST, STONED ON GRASS THROUGHOUT ENTIRE SERIES.

~~Miss~~ Lozano's work has been shown in the 31st Biennial Exhibition at the Corcoran Gallery of Art in Washington, D. C., '69 at Bennington College, '66 (SHOW) and in other galleries. GREEN & BIANCHINI (SHOW, 66) IN NYC, RICKE (SHOW, '69) IN COLOGNE, GERMANY. ~~Her work is currently on exhibition at the Ricke Gallery in Cologne, Germany.~~

~~A native of~~ BORN IN Newark, N. J., NOV. 5, '30, 4:25 PM (APPROX) Lee Lozano ~~received~~ her B. A. degree at the University of Chicago, '48-'51 ~~and a~~ B. F. A. from ~~the~~ Art Institute of Chicago. '56-'60 Her studio ~~is~~ in New York.

IDENTITY: NOV 5, '30, APPROX 4:25 PM, NEWARK, N.J.
PRESENT NAME: LEE LOZANO
\# \# \# SCHOOLS: UNIV. OF CHICAGO, '48-'51, B.A.
ART INST. OF ", '56-'60, B.F.A.

FOR ~~INFORMATION~~ ABOUT THE FUTURE, RAP WITH THE ARTIST.
For ~~further~~ info~~rmation:~~ ABOUT THE PAST Leon Levine: 249-4100 (PUBLIC RELATIONS)
Romi Roland

PANEL IN SERIES	NO. OF WAVES	WAVELENGTH	LENGTH OF PAINTING SESSION FOR WAVEAREA *	DATE FINISHED		COLOR
1	2	48"	8 HRS	MAR 12, 68		2 COLORS
2	4	24"	8 "	DEC 16, 67		" "
3	6	16"	9 "	{FEB 5, 68 * {MAY 16, 70		" "
4	8	12"	10 "	FEB 16, 69		" "
5	12	8"	12 "	MAY 9, 68		" "
6	16	6"	14 "	JAN 15, 69		" "
7	24	4"	18 "	MAR 19 ?, 69	(NOTE LOSS OF INTEREST IN KEEPING RECORDS)	MONOCHROME *
8	32	3"	24 "	JULY 26, 69		"
9	48	2"	2 DAYS	FALL, 69		"
10	96	1"	3 "	1970 ?		"
11	192	½"	—	(UNFINISHED)		—

*CONTINUOUS, I.E., NO BREAKS LONGER THAN A COUPLE HOURS

*ORIGINAL VERSION OF 6-WAVE DESTROYED DUE TO BAD COLOR (SEE SAMPLE FOR TOUCHING)

* ADDING A 2ND COLOR ON ONE EDGE OF WAVEAREA WHILE PAINT STILL WET BECAME TOO DIFFICULT

Whitney Museum press release with Lozano's notes, 1970

Waves at the Whitney

The eleven canvases comprising the *Wave* series were meant to represent the extended electromagnetic spectrum. Lozano's plan was to make visible what is usually invisible through a metaphor—"metaphor" being used here not in a rhetorical sense, but rather in a strictly etymological one: to transfer or carry a concept from one field (invisible reality) into another (artistic/scientific language). Her scientific starting point was a dry infographic from *Great Ideas and Theories of Modern Cosmology* by Jagjit Singh (1961). Her artistic process entailed a visual endeavor that was also, or perhaps primarily, an energetic one. Lozano acted as an agent for the metaphorical process to unfold. Indeed, on the press release issued by the Whitney Museum, she crossed out the evocative, verbose description drafted by the institution, opting to focus on the technical information relevant to the experiment: medium, principle, expected result, and the state of the artist (stoned on grass throughout the series). Below, she added a chart offering further relevant data: the number of waves for each canvas (2, 4, 6, 8, 12, 16, 24, 32, 48, 96, 192—constituent even factors derived by dividing the vertical dimension of each canvas, 96 inches), and the duration of the painting session (each painting was produced in one sitting, with no breaks longer than two hours, even in the case of the final canvas, which took her fifty-two hours).

When she exhibited the series in her solo show at the Whitney Museum of American Art (December 2, 1970–January 3, 1971), she decided to augment the main installation with two additional elements. The first was a piece of canvas cut from the first version of the *6 Wave*, which she had ended up destroying "due to bad color."

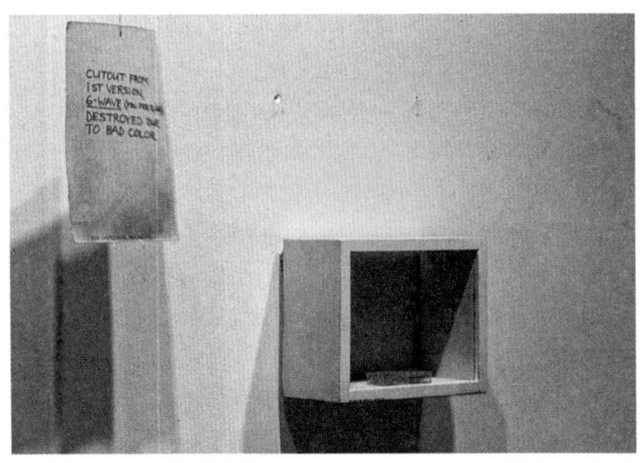

Installation view, *Lee Lozano*, Whitney Museum
of American Art, New York, 1970–71

Next to it, on a shelf, she displayed a nearly forgotten
body of work, the *Me Pieces*, consisting of small transparent
plastic boxes containing body hair, nail clippings, and other
bodily waste. This odd sculptural intervention stood as
a (different type of) testimony to the energy she released
into the project, data she might have decided to record
in case it proved to be relevant when looking back at the
overall results of the experiment. It also had a documentary
value, indicating the time spent pursuing her efforts:
If the paintings were the visual results of the experience,
these bodily by-products were its physical outcomes.
The registration of the passing of time was the direct effect
of a shift in her perspective toward her work. As she had
realized a few months earlier, "my art is about t.! I'll leave
space/matter to the sculptor experts." Time was entering
aggressively into the picture, the first three dimensions not
being sufficient anymore for the kind of work Lozano was
aiming at. The revelation came, as often, through a pun.
A few pages earlier, she had written, "I don't get spaced
on dope, I get timed."

　　　　　　　　　Materials and Making

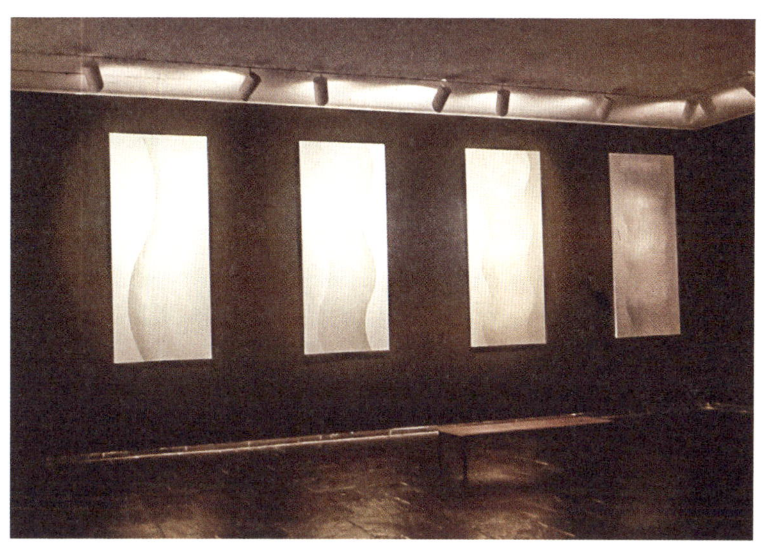

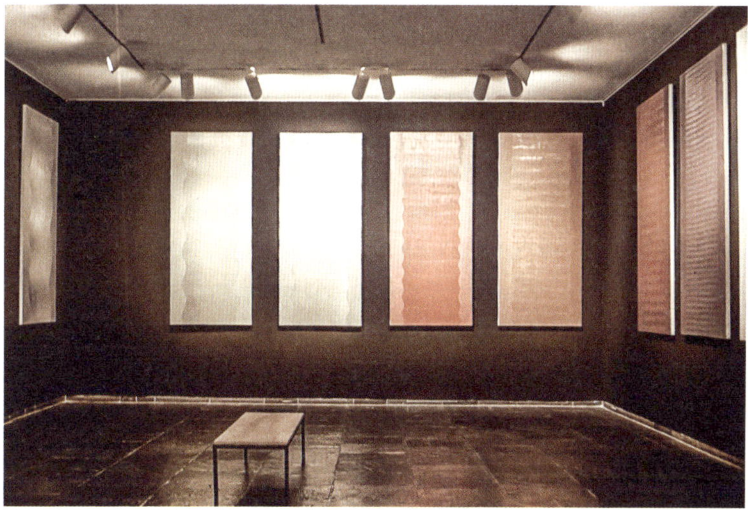

Installation views, *Lee Lozano*, Whitney Museum of American Art, New York, 1970–71

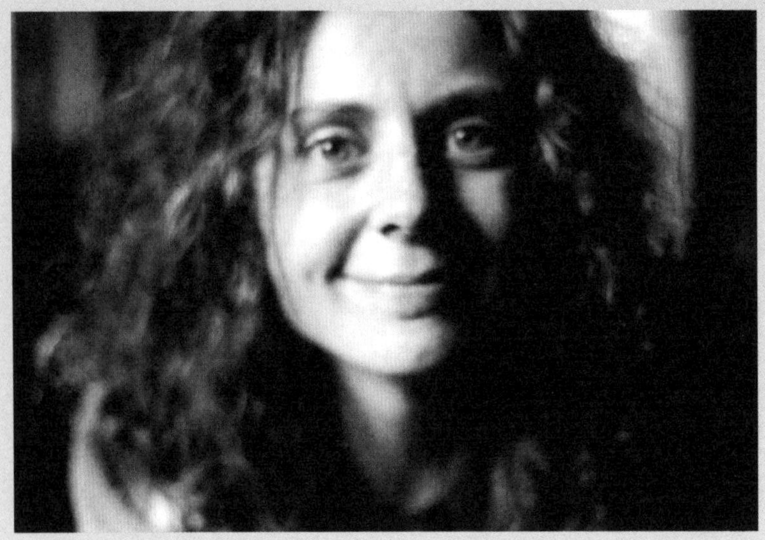

Acid Trip, Halifax (3-State experiment), 1971

Lozano and Drugs

Lozano's drug use was often overlooked, judged moralistically, or dismissed as a relatively common recreational activity in the late 1960s. However, for her, drug consumption was an extremely frequent and carefully executed practice, often pursued with specific intentions and explored as a legitimate transformative process for one's body, perspective, and behavior. Lozano frequently employed certain drugs as tools in her thinking process. Psychedelics, in particular, played a pivotal role in providing profound insights into reality and art, one of which led to her revelation of the supremacy of painting over sculpture: "as a result of the multi-dimensionality of the acid experience which renders thought-process into spectacular supra-sculptural forms unhampered by the need for support or by the force of gravity, whose process is edge-of-universe time-energy and whose material is quarkite, the man-made sculpture of this earth becomes weary, stale and flat. Not real enough, not lie enough. How abstract, absolved and absolute is the lie of painting! no other here-artform approaches the honesty with which painting tells its lie."

Conversely, marijuana played a central role in determining the state in which she would work. The effects of being stoned on her creative process were rigorously tested and analyzed, particularly through her *Grass Piece* and *No-Grass Piece*, culminating in the realization that "Both grass & no-grass states produce fantasy which is the breeding ground for more formalized thoughts. Fantasy and mind-wandering seem indispensable if ya wanna keep movin'." In 1969 she theorized the *SDS Piece*, consisting of the creation of three identical paintings while stoned, drunk, and sober. A version of this concept was put into practice in 1971 when she delivered an eight-hour-long lecture at the Nova Scotia College of Art and Design titled "The Halifax 3 State Experiment" (pp. 112–13). Spanning multiple locations, Lozano gave the lecture while sober, stoned, and high on LSD. The conflation of her work with altered states of consciousness was crucial to her attempt to disrupt habitual patterns, heighten perception, and ultimately achieve—and possibly share—a form of enlightenment.

LOZANO

APRIL 10, 1969

STATEMENT FOR OPEN PUBLIC HEARING,
ART WORKERS COALITION.

FOR ME THERE CAN BE NO ART REVOLUTION
THAT IS SEPARATE FROM A SCIENCE
REVOLUTION, A POLITICAL REVOLUTION,
AN EDUCATION REVOLUTION, A DRUG
REVOLUTION, A SEX REVOLUTION OR A
PERSONAL REVOLUTION. I CANNOT CONSIDER
A PROGRAM OF MUSEUM REFORMS WITHOUT
EQUAL ATTENTION TO GALLERY REFORMS
AND ART MAGAZINE REFORMS WHICH WOULD
AIM TO ELIMINATE STABLES OF ARTISTS
AND WRITERS. I WILL NOT CALL MYSELF
AN ART WORKER BUT RATHER AN ART
DREAMER AND I WILL PARTICIPATE ONLY
IN A TOTAL REVOLUTION SIMULTANEOUSLY
PERSONAL AND PUBLIC.

LEE LOZANO
60 GRAND ST., N.Y.C.

Statement for Open Public Hearing, Art Workers' Coalition, April 10, 1969

Personal and Public Revolution

During the years Lozano was in New York, the United States saw large-scale anti-war protests, civil rights marches, boycotts, and a burgeoning feminist movement. Many artists lent their support to these causes, participating in protests and staging benefit exhibitions, while also turning their attention toward the structural inequities marring the art world. Lozano attended meetings held by the Art Workers' Coalition and early feminist gatherings. Though she was sympathetic to their concerns, Lozano ultimately rejected collective political activity. Nonetheless, the political climate of the time influenced her thinking and activity—especially major works such as *General Strike Piece*, *Dialogue Piece*, *Dropout Piece*, and her decision to boycott women.

The Art Workers' Coalition

According to Lozano, her "Life-Art" pieces were part of her quest for a "personal and public revolution." Her pseudo-political manifesto was articulated in her *General Strike Piece*, in which she announced her progressive withdrawal from art events in order to pursue her revolutionary ends. This strike can also be understood within the broader political climate of the time. Indeed, Lozano herself suggested referring to a statement she had read at an open public hearing held by the newly founded Art Workers' Coalition (AWC), to better understand the terms of her "revolution." The AWC was a group of artists, curators, and other art workers, many of them Lozano's friends and acquaintances, which had come together in January to protest the mistreatment of artists and art workers in museums. Among other issues, they denounced the underrepresentation of artists who did not fall under the category of white male in institutional programs and criticized the way institutions and commercial galleries exploited artists' work. These topics were not foreign to Lozano, who was well known for being critical of the system. Indeed, she herself had called for the boycott of galleries and dealers in her notebooks just a few months earlier (pp. 85–86), fantasizing about possible new ways to evaluate artwork, and proposing a utopian system in which artists would be the ones rating collectors, who would exist purely for the entertainment of artists.

The open hearing followed weeks of negotiations between the AWC and the Museum of Modern Art's director, Bates Lowry, the campaign's primary target, to whom the AWC had submitted a list of thirteen demands. The meeting was called "What Should Be the Program of the Art Workers Regarding Museum Reform, and to Establish the Program of the Art Workers' Coalition" and took place at the School of Visual Arts on April 10, 1969. Three hundred or so people attended, and statements were submitted by many. Among them were Dan Graham, with whom Lozano was in a romantic relationship; her close friends Hollis Frampton and Carl Andre; and Lucy Lippard, with whom Lozano was collaborating at the time. Despite all indications suggesting a vision perfectly in tune with theirs, Lozano's statement struck a note of rupture. She proclaimed: "For me there can be no art revolution that is separate from a science revolution, a political revolution, an education revolution, a drug revolution, a sex revolution or a personal revolution." According to Lozano, the reformist approach of her peers was not enough to fix the system's issues, whose roots ran deep in society at large.

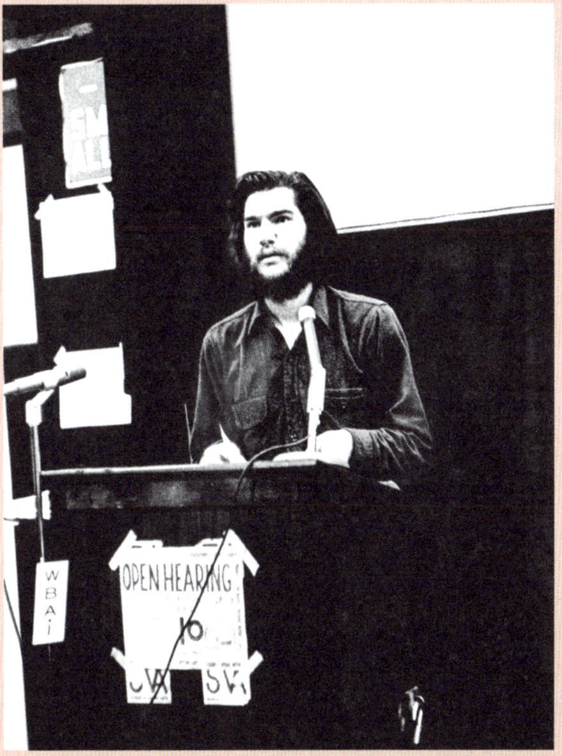

Dan Graham speaking at the AWC Open Hearing, 1969

Fake Museum
of Modern Art
membership
pass, designed
by conceptual artist
Joseph Kosuth for
the AWC, 1969

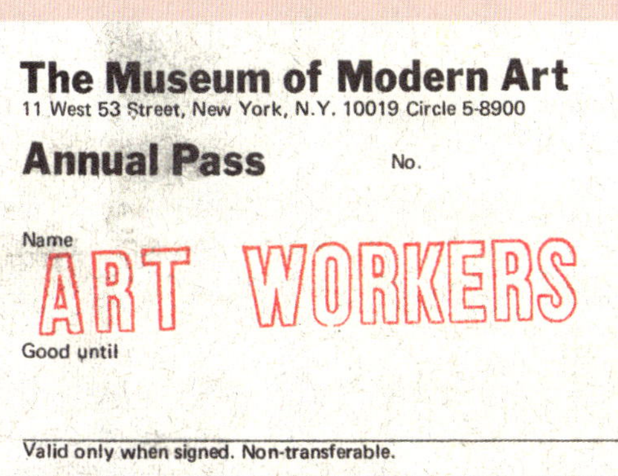

Lozano had a similarly conflicted—if not outright adversarial—relationship with the feminist circles emerging at the time. Lozano's obstinacy in claiming her own space in a deeply male-dominated field and her successful refusal of societal expectations aligned her with the feminist movement's rejection of patriarchal rule. In her notebooks, Lozano often encouraged others to follow suit: "Women have been tricked into thinking that whelping is their fulfillment . . . Women, refuse to have children! Develop your minds, learn more about the universe." Her scandalous lifestyle and devoted exploration of her own sexuality and pleasure could have sparked rewarding conversations in feminist circles, where concepts such as the objectification of women's bodies and the male gaze were in the process of being elaborated, anticipating a new vision of female sexuality that focused on clitoridean rather than vaginal pleasure. Yet, while many of Lozano's ethical concerns and positions aligned with the broader agenda of second-wave feminism, her approach remained distinct, highly individualistic, and, finally, oppositional.

Indeed, Lozano's call for a "total personal and public revolution" resonated with the feminist slogan "the personal is political," even if it differed in intent. While feminist movements sought to bridge the gap between the private and public spheres in order to come together and make visible the collective nature of the structural violence women faced in their private lives, Lozano's struggle ultimately involved no one but herself. She was fundamentally allergic to systematic forms of organization and group definitions and activities. Furthermore, feminist groups at the time were gathering in an attempt to create a new subjectivity, language, and identity—one that would no longer be defined in opposition or relation to the male paradigm. To do so, men could not be invited to the meetings, and, for Lozano, separatism was a problem. After years of resisting gendered constraints to establish herself as an equal among men, she was now confronted with the demand to embrace her identity as a woman. To her, this felt like a regression. She found the feminist meetings she attended to be uninspiring and stifling. The feminist movement, for Lozano, was not a space of liberation but one that imposed its own set of boundaries—a contradiction she could not reconcile. "I am not a feminist. I speak to both men and women because both are slaves in today's society," she insisted. Lozano's dissatisfaction with the movement grew until it dramatically burst into *Boycott Women* in 1971.

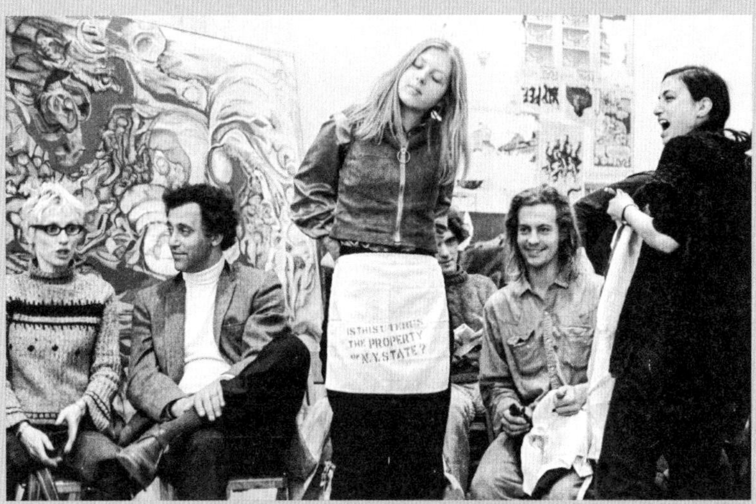

Poppy Johnson (center) at a joint Women Artists in Revolution and AWC meeting, New York, 1970

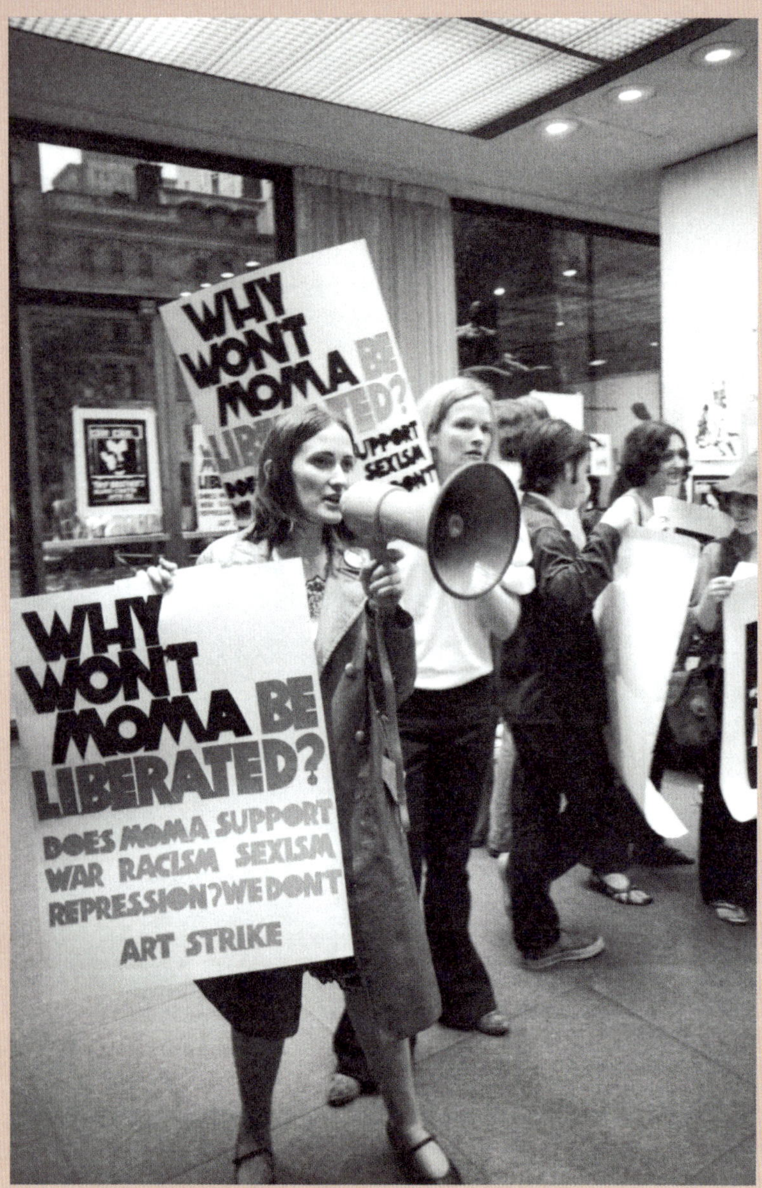

Protesters at the Museum of Modern Art, New York, 1970

                    Cultural Context

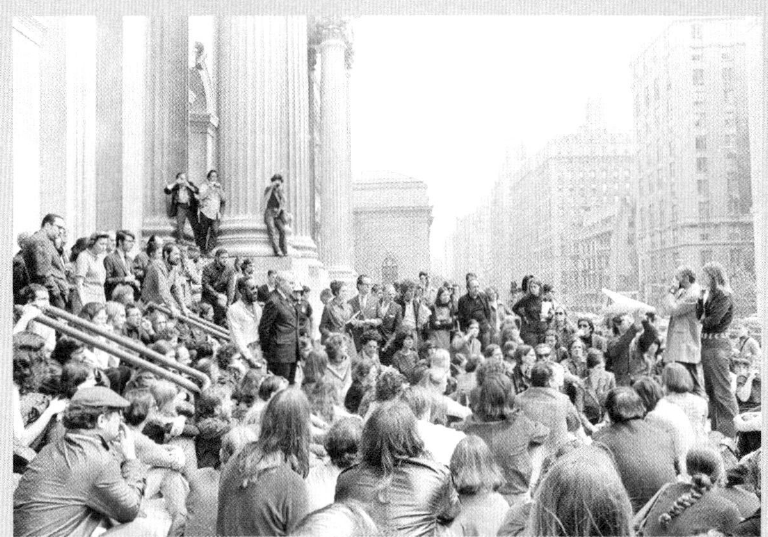

Robert Morris speaking at a protest on the steps of the Metropolitian Museum of Art, New York, 1970

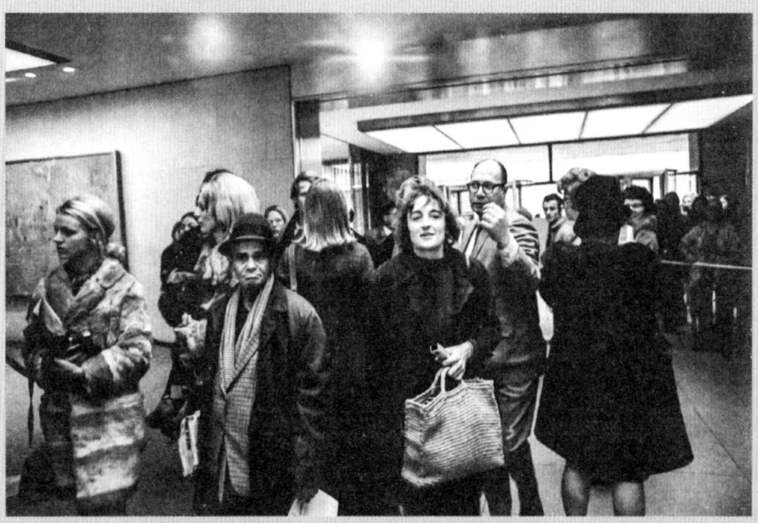

Lucy Lippard and members of the AWC protesting at the Museum of Modern Art, New York, 1971

FOR THEIR AUDIENCE.

ARTFORUM AD IDEAS:

Private Book 5, 1970, p. 89

Dropping Out

The months leading up to the Whitney Museum opening found Lozano increasingly disillusioned with the art scene. Its competition, nepotism, and hypocrisy are recurring themes in her notebooks, where she raged against "artpigs & artrats" and responded to the art world's issues with dedicated pieces. Some of these aimed to directly tackle practical problems, such as the *Lozano Emergency T.S. * Fund (LETSF) (*tough shit you're out of cash)* (p. 28), where "LETSF" stands for "let's fuck." Others sarcastically mocked prescribed authorities, as in *Throwing Up Piece*: "Throw the last 12 issues of Artforum up in the air"—a deliberate play on the double meaning of "throw up." At the same time, Lozano was making her work increasingly resistant to commodification, planning strict limitations on the sale of her paintings and dispersing her "Life-Art"

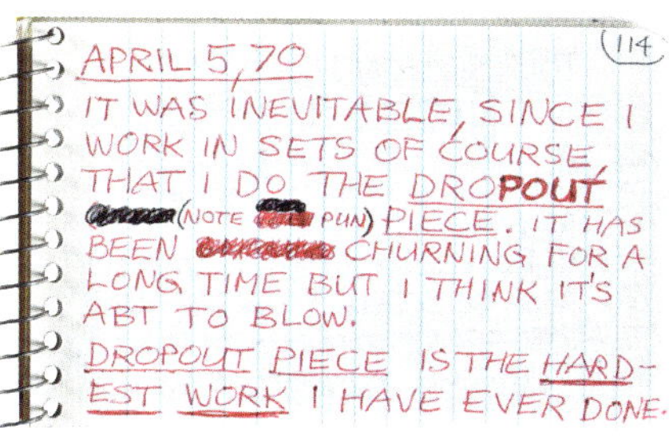

Private Book 8, April 5, 1970, pp. 114–16

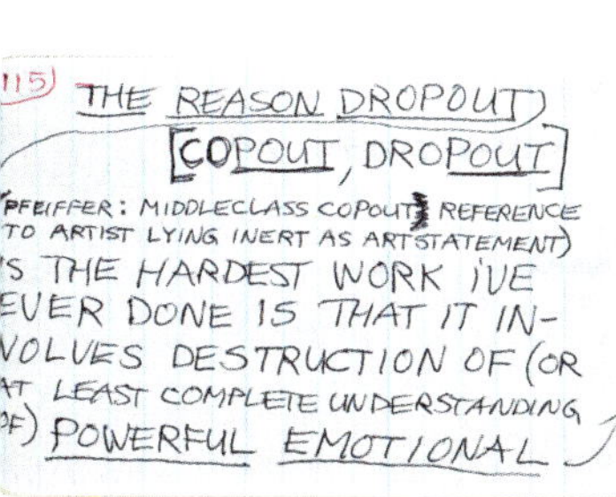

No title (detail), 1970. Ink on paper, 9 × 11 in. (22.9 × 27.9 cm)

pieces across different versions and formats. This aligned with her conviction that "ideas are the most powerful thing in the world" and her belief in their free circulation: "Pass (piss? watch out!) on ideas. Nevermind who gets the credit for them, you rival rabbits" (p. 111). We don't know whether these proposals failed to generate enough enthusiasm, but we do know that Lozano marked her ten-year anniversary in the city with a bitter realization: "NYC: a decade of competitiveness. Where competition thrives, friends can't exist." The overall review of her life in the city up to that moment was crowned with a sketch for a possible advertisement for her Whitney show, consisting of a photo portraying herself naked, preferably having sex, captioned with the slogan "servicing the art world for ten years!" (p. 106).

In perfect alignment with Lozano's motto, "Win first don't last, win last don't care," the preparation for her most important exhibition to date coincided with the premeditation of her final dropout from the very system that was about to glorify her. On April 5, 1970, a few months before the opening, Lozano noted: "It was inevitable, since I work in sets of course, that I do the <u>Dropout</u> (note pun) <u>Piece</u>. It has been churning for a long time but I think it's abt to blow." Even though it was framed as logical—and inevitable—*Dropout Piece* introduced radically new, unprecedented elements into her practice. While actions such as withdrawals, strikes, and boycotts implied an antagonistic yet still relational stance, *Dropout* signified an absolute, irreversible act of departure. Indeed, Lozano continued, "<u>Dropout Piece</u> is the <u>hardest work</u> I have ever done. <u>The reason dropout</u> is the hardest work I've ever done is that it involves destruction of (or at least complete understanding of) <u>powerful emotional habits</u>. <u>Key</u> → <u>emotions are also habits</u>, like any other repetitive behavior. I want to get over my habit of emotional dependence on love. I want to start trusting myself & others more. I want to really believe that I have power & complete my own fate" (p. 107). Consistent with her practice up to that point—and probably more than in any previous instance—art, existence, and an in-depth reflection on the systems regulating both, were not distinguishable in Lozano's words. Even if it was framed as a "piece" and listed in continuity with works that had the art system as their starting point, *Dropout Piece* was not only (or not really) about the art world. It was first and foremost about her own independence.

In Lozano's philosophical framework, habits fostered dependence—on things, emotions, and values. In her practice, she worked to dismantle conventional behaviors, questioning the systems of power that imposed them, and carving out space for unforeseen possibilities: "Start living at more <u>random</u> hours. Destroy schedules.

Sleep, eat, groom, take vitamin pills etc <u>irregularly</u> to build up resistance to <u>habit-forming</u>, to make living more interesting & flexible." Her battles extended further, challenging established notions of gender, labor, power, and fame, either by directly confronting them or by subtly withdrawing from the roles she was expected to perform. In 1968 she articulated her position with clarity: "Some <u>institutions</u> I do not believe in: onanism, domination, slavery, competition, winning, marriage, the family, parenthood, patriarchy, matriarchy, possession, security, food, god, hierarchy." Refusing to comply with all of that was, in itself, a labor-intensive endeavor. Her disciplined documentation of her daily transactions—whether related to food, sex, drugs, social interactions, or work—functioned as both a safeguard against habit formation and a method of self-surveillance, a tool to exert control over her own behavioral patterns.

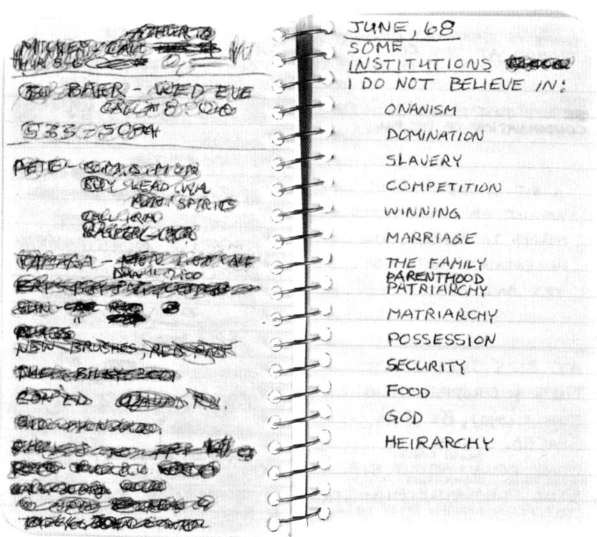

Private Book I, June 1968, pp. 58–59

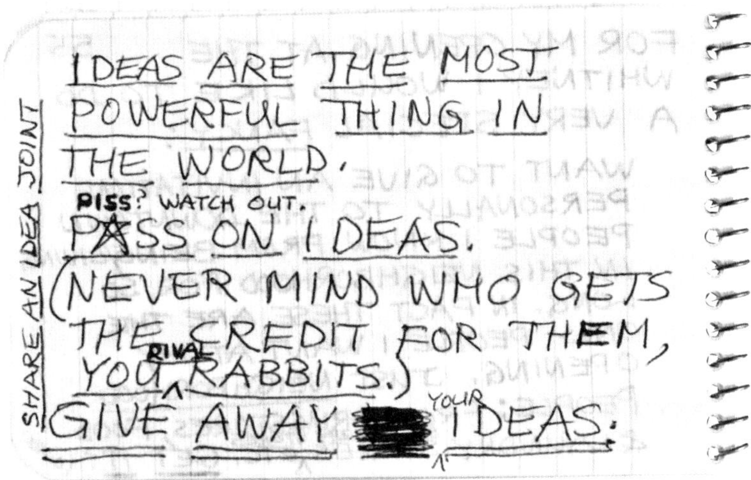

Private Book 6, 1970, p. 55

Dropout Piece signaled that her system was beginning to fail, as it allowed for dependencies that increasingly threatened her freedom: "<u>Dropout</u> only works along with <u>diminished consumption</u>: of calories, cigs, dope; of joyous energy (like dancing), emotions, intensity; of restlessness, ambition, work." The choice of using the definition of "consumption" in this context is significant: Lozano was aware of the pervasive, capitalist-driven commodification that seeped into every facet of life—art included, the system being hardly a sanctuary. Positioned simultaneously as both a product and consumer, she sought to reclaim agency over the very mechanisms through which desire was constructed.

Lecture at the Nova Scotia College of Art and Design, Halifax

This excerpt is from a lecture Lozano delivered to students on July 16, 1971. The audio recording from which this transcript was made is one of the only existing documents of Lozano speaking and offers a rare insight into her public voice.

That brings me to other differences, differences in life events and the kind of abstractions we get involved in. For example, what is expected of an artist or any creative person, as opposed to what really happens? Everyone knows that an artist's best work often covers a very short period of time, yet the artist is expected to function on a high, high level of performance at all times. If that artist does very good at one period in life, he or she is always actually competing with their own great period of works. It's almost always very rare that an artist does high quality work and maintains this great period throughout their career. Yet, its expected of him. And there's some contrast there. I talked to some mathematicians recently and I brought this question up. Mathematics is a field in which the creative person, the mathematician, often reaches a very high peak of inventiveness/creativeness with his work at a young age. I asked one of the mathematicians, what was expected of them. And he said it the same as you describe with what's expected in art. A mathematician is supposed to maintain forever the high quality in the work that he does, even though it's known this doesn't happen very often and any place he appears, he'll be asked, well, what are you working on now, what's your big idea now. . . . There's somehow discrepancy there now between what really exists and what is expected.

The Artist's Voice

This leads me to the concept of competition. Does this
state of what is expected from a person, does this involve
competitiveness? I've always said that if you do hit a
high period in your work you are actually competing with
yourself in a way, but what about competition between
each other, within your own field? I've seen some very
destructive acts occur between artists—viciousness, desire
to cut people out, all kinds of trouble occur. I must say that
the mathematicians do take care of each other. I didn't see
that [competition] going on. I get very concerned that this
doesn't happen in the art world. . . . I'd just like to bring up
a point on competition to make you aware of it. I think that
a kind of dignity should be expected. I'm talking from a
point of view when you are out of school, although these
things happen in school when you're really competing
(there's that word again) with other artists in a place like
New York or elsewhere. I've been saying [that] there are
some colleges with very fine reputations that as much
as anything, I think, teach social games and competitive
games, competitive techniques, in fact, I went so far as
to say that some of the worst elements of society graduate
from places like Andover, Bennington, Yale . . . or Harvard.
The idea has upset a lot of people when I say the worst
elements of society and dangerous programs, competitive
ideas are bred in places like that. I don't know how much
we need competition to survive, I just want to talk about it,
I want to get it out, you know?

Dialogue Piece, 1969

In 1969, Lozano began *Dialogue Piece*, which seemingly
contradicted the more isolating *General Strike Piece*,
commenced the previous fall. To realize *Dialogue Piece*,
Lozano invited people to her loft for the specific purpose
of having a conversation. She recorded the dates, people
involved, and sometimes the quality of the exchange
in a notebook, though the content of the conversations
remained private. Nauseated by the competition triggered
by the social arena of gallery openings, and skeptical
toward the restrictive context of organized collectives,
Lozano preferred to meet her peers—and have them
meet her work—one on one, in her own "crib." Notably,
the moment when Lozano began inviting people over
coincided with her second thoughts about publicly
displaying the *Waves* series, which, still in her studio,
happened to be the backdrop for her conversations.
The transition of her social interactions from public
to private was aligned with her reluctance to detach
broader political discourse from personal existence,
just as art could not be separated from life. At the
same time, it signaled how Lozano might have started
to envision the possibility of non-return. In July, in an
almost prophetic moment of self-awareness, her notebook
records a question that seems to seal her final decision:
"The dialogues are a saying goodbye?"

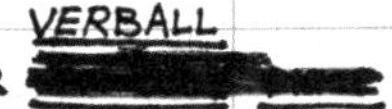

~~[struck-out line]~~

IT WAS A CONGENIAL MEETING & WAS ONLY OCCASIONALLY BROKEN BY SMALL FARTS.... _SCREW_, THE WEEKLY SEX REVIEW.

DIALOGUE PIECE (STARTED APRIL 21, 69) OR ~~[struck out]~~

CALL (OR WRITE) [SPEAK TO] PEOPLE FOR THE SPECIFIC PURPOSE OF INVITING THEM TO YR LOFT FOR A DIALOGUE. IN PROCESS FOR THE REST OF "LIFE".

APRIL 21, 69 — CALL MOOSE (ROBT MORRIS). LEAVE NAME & NUMBER WITH HIS ANSWERING SERVICE.

MAY 11, 69 — CALL WALTER DEMARIA. LEAVE NAME ONLY WITH A.S.

MAY 13, 69 — CALL WALTER DE MARIA. LEAVE NAME & NO. WITH A.S.

MAY 14, 69 — CALL JAP (JASPER JOHNS) AT CASTELLI GALLERY. LEAVE NAME & NO. WITH DAVID WHITE WHO PROMISES TO GET MESSAGE TO JAP ALTHO JAP IS "VERY BUSY & IN & OUT OF TOWN THIS WEEK".

MAY 14, 69 — CALL POONSIE (LARRY POONS). HE ANSWERS PHONE, WE MAKE A DATE FOR MAY 21 (WED.), 4 P.M.

NOTE: START ~~RECORDING OF~~ [WRITE-UP OF] PIECE WHEN YOU HAVE MADE THE FIRST "CONTACT." SO FAR THE PEOPLE CALLED ARE THOSE WITH WHOM A DIALOGUE HAS ALREADY BEEN STARTED IN THE "PAST", A DIALOGUE WHICH MIGHT BE INTERESTING TO "PURSUE."

MAY 16, 69 — MOOSE RET'NS MY CALL. WE MAKE DATE FOR MAY 17 (SAT), 5 P.M.

MAY 17, 69 — MOOSE VISITS, THEN WE GO TO HIS CRIB, TURN ON & HAVE A GREAT DIALOGUE, THAT IS, A LONG INTENSE TALK WITHOUT TOO MUCH TENSION DURING WHICH WE EXCHANGE MANY IDEAS.

NOTE: THE PURPOSE OF THIS PIECE IS TO ~~TALK TO~~ [HAVE A DIALOGUE WITH AS MANY] PEOPLE [AS POSS.], NOT TO MAKE A PIECE. ANY PERSONAL INFORMATION EXCHANGED DURING DIALOGUE WILL BE PROTECTED BY MY CONFIDENCE. IF ANYONE WISHES IDEAS TO BE PASSED ON ~~TO OTHER PEOPLE~~ I SHALL COMPLY, AS MUCH AS POSS.

MAY 18 — CALL JOHN GIORNO, LEAVE/NAME & NO. W/A.S.

" — CALL CLAUS OLDENBURG. SPEAK TO PATTY WHO WILL PASS MESSAGE ON TO CLAUS WHEN HE GETS BACK TO N.Y. IN 2 WKS.

" — CALL YVONNE RAINER. WE MAKE DATE FOR SUN, MAY 25, WILL CALL.

" — CALL MY MOTHER, WHO IS ILL. SHE IS HAVING FIRST DRUG EXPERIENCE & I INVITE HER TO HAVE DIALOGUE BY LONG-DIST. PHONE.

" — ATTEND OPENING OF LUCY'S SHOW AT PAULA COOPER'S. SPEAK TO AT LEAST 13 PEOPLE WHOM I'LL CALL FOR A DIALOGUE.

~~NOTE: "DIALOGUE": AN EXCHANGE BETWEEN TWO PEOPLE, THE FORM OF WHICH NEED NOT BE LIMITED TO VERBAL.~~

Dialogue Piece (part one), 1969. Ink on paper, 11 × 8½ in. (27.9 × 21.6 cm)

DIALOGUE PIECE (CONTINUED) (P.41)

MAY 19,69 – JOHN GIORNO RET'NS CALL, WILL CALL WED OR THUR.

  "   "   – CALL HEIZER TO ACKNOWLEDGE REC'T OF REPROS, INVITE HIM FOR DIALOGUE, HE'LL CALL SOON & BRING MORE PRINTS TO SHOW ME.

  "   "   – CALL IAN WILSON, LEAVE NAM/NO. W/HIS WIFE?

  "   20,69 – DAVID LEE CALLS FROM DOWNSTAIRS, WAKING ME UP & WE HAVE BEAUTIFUL TWO HOUR DIALOGUE (BEFORE I EVEN HAVE A CHANCE TO TAKE A SHIT).

  "   "   – IAN WILSON RETURNS CALL. AFTER A VERY UNPLEASANT CONVERSATION HE REFUSES TO VISIT. I SUGGEST TAKING A WALK, HE REFUSES & CAN'T WAIT TO GET OFF PHONE. THE CONVERSATION YIELDED AN ENORMOUS AMOUNT OF INFORMATION, IN SPITE OF HIS BEING ADAMANT ABOUT NOT BELIEVING IN "PASSING INFORMATION," AND SOME OF HIS QUESTIONS FORCED ME TO THINK MORE ABOUT WHAT I AM DOING. HE PUT HIS IDEAS INTO ART MAG JARGON: "ARE YOU SETTING UP AN ENVIRONMENT?" HE SAID SOMETHING ABOUT THE FIRST "CONVERSATION" WE HAD (ABT A YR AGO, AT LONGVIEW, THRU LUCY'S SUGGESTING THAT HE TALK TO ME), THAT IT MADE HIM VOMIT, OR SOMETHING WE "TALKED" ABOUT CONCERNING ART MAGS WHICH I DON'T RECALL. I MUST NOW DECIDE WHAT TO "DO".

(NOTE: MENTION INVITING AN ANIMAL TO I.W. DURING THIS CALL.)

MAY 21 – NO WORD FROM POONSIE, CALL HIM AT 5:15 P.M. HE SAID (A BIT FAKELY) "OH THIS IS WEDNESDAY ISN'T IT", THAT HE WAS "INTA SUMPTHIN", COULD I CALL NEXT TUES, I SAID I'D BE GLAD TO CALL NEXT WEEK, AND HE CALLED ME "DEAR".

/ MAY 22 – JOHN TORREANO CALLS, I INVITE HIM OVER & WE HAVE DIALOGUE ON GRASS HE BROUGHT. AT END HE STAYS TOO LONG BUT THEN I AM SO TIRED, I WOULD NOT HAVE BEEN "UP" TO ANYTHING TODAY. IT WAS GOOD DIALOGUE, VERY "DENSE," I CLARIFIED SOME IMPORTANT IDEAS.

DECIDE TO INVITE A CAT & A BABY FOR A DIALOGUE EACH. (MAY 22, 69)

MAY 23 – CALL LARRY WEINER (AS I PROMISED AT COOPER OPENING). MAKE DATE FOR VISIT MON, MAY 26, 4 P.M.

/ MAY 24 – KALTENBACH COMES AT LAST FOR OUR FIRST "OFFICIAL" DIALOGUE. WE TRADE A LOT OF OUR ART IDEAS & DISCUSS DOING A PIECE TOGETHER WHEN HE RETURNS FROM CAL. (HE LEAVES ON JUNE 3 FOR SUMMER TEACHING JOB).

Dialogue Piece (part two), 1969. Ink on paper, 11 × 8½ in. (27.9 × 21.6 cm)

DIALOGUE PIECE (CONTINUED) (P.42)

MAY 24, 69 WHEN I CALL CLAIRE COPLEY TO APOLOGIZE FOR ABRUPT DEPARTURE LAST NIGHT FROM LA MONTE'S I INVITE HER & WE MAKE DATE FOR WED, MAY 28, AFTER 7 P.M.

" 25 CALL YVONNE AROUND 2 P.M., NO ANSWER. AGAIN LATER (TO BE CORRECT) AT 6:15. NO ANSWER.

" 25 CALL DAVID DIAO, HE'LL CALL VERY SOON FOR A VISIT.

/ " 25 CALL ALAN SARET, HE WILL COME TONIGHT AT 9:00. LATER: IT WAS A VERY SLUGGISH DIALOGUE BUT I LEARN MORE THAN CAN BE EXPRESSED VERBALLY FROM ALAN (A LOT ABT HIS NO-SCENE), AND ABOUT THIS TIME & PLACE IN HISTORY. ALSO REALIZE I HAVE NO FLOOR-PAD FOR STONED GUESTS' STRETCHING OUT.

/ " 26 LARRY WEINER & I HAVE A "FAST-PACED" DIALOGUE. HE SEEMS TO BEHAVE AS THOUGH TO LET THE OTHER PERSON TALK IS TO LET THE OTHER PERSON WIN. THE "ELEMENT" MISSING FROM THIS DIALOGUE WHICH HAPPENED TO BE PRESENT IN ALL THE PREVIOUS DIALOGUES WAS <u>LOVE</u>.

/ " 28 CLAIRE COPLEY MOSTLY TALKS DURING DIALOGUE, ~~SEEMS MOST~~ IS INTERESTED IN LEARNING, SHE SAID.

/ " 30 DAN GRAHAM & I HAVE IMPORTANT DIALOGUE IN THAT DEFINITE CHANGES WERE IMMEDIATELY EFFECTED BECAUSE OF IT.

JUNE 2, 69 CALL POONS, LEAVE NAME & NO. W/A.S.

" " CALL BRICE, MAKE DATE FOR JUNE 3 (TUE), 8:30. WILL BRICE MARDEN BRING HIS OLD LADY, I WONDER?

/ " 3 NO, BRICE DOESN'T COME WITH HELEN & WE HAVE DIALOGUE ABOUT "THE REVO-LUTION", BRICE TALKING ALMOST ENTIRELY ABT SHITTY BUSINESS PRACTICES IN THE ART WORLD, & SHITTY TREATMENT OF ARTISTS BY EACH OTHER.

/ " 4 LARRY STAFFORD WHO IS IN BLDG TO VISIT RAY SIEMANOWSKI KNOCKS ON MY DOOR & WE HAVE SPONTANEOUS DIALOGUE, MUCH ABT GALLERY & DEALER PITFALLS.

" 5&6 ALAN SARET RETURNS BOTH THESE NIGHTS & WE CONTINUE DIALOGUE. MORE LATER RE THIS.

// " 6 —> VOGELS VISIT, WE HAVE LONG "DIALOGUE."

/ " 7 SERRA COMES OVER A LITTLE HIGH ON BEER & NO FOOD. JUST INTO A DIALOGUE WITH HIM (WE'VE BEEN SMOKING SARET'S HASH) WHEN HE GETS AN ATTACK (TOO STONED), FALLS OFF CHAIR TO FLOOR WITH A CRASH, HAS "CONVULSIONS" & PASSES OUT. LATER HE FEELS SICK, LIES DOWN ON BED UNTIL SARET COMES OVER.

" 9 CALL MORE PEOPLE FOR DIALOGUE. FROM NOW ON I WON'T ENTER THESE CALLS IN <u>PIECE</u> BUT ONLY DIALOGUES PER SE, & CALLS WHEN THEY ARE RELEVANT.

/ " 10 MEET WITH DICK ANDERSON. WE WALK TO 8TH ST. BKSTORES & RETURN TO HIS LOFT FOR REST OF "DIALOGUE". HE TALKS CONTINUOUSLY.

Dialogue Piece (part three), 1969. Ink on paper, 11 × 8½ in. (27.9 × 21.6 cm)

DIALOGUE PIECE (CONTINUED)(p.43)

/ JUNE 16, 69 — GARY BOWER COMES FOR DIALOGUE AT 3:00 P.M. & LEAVES
AT 9:00 P.M. IT WAS ENGAGING ALMOST THE WHOLE TIME.

/ " 17 — GARY STEVENS TALKS ABT HIS JOB AT MENTAL HOSP. &
OTHER INTERESTING SUBJECTS BUT I SENSE SOMETHING
(RESISTANCE, TENSION)? ████████ WHICH KEEPS HIM AT
A DISTANCE. PERHAPS HE WAS JUST UNCOMFORTABLE?

" 18 — SEND FOLLOWING POSTCARD TO WALTER DE MARIA: THE REASON I
CALLED YOU TWICE TO WHICH YOU HAVE NOT BEEN GRACIOUS
ENOUGH TO REPLY WAS TO INVITE YOU FOR A DIALOGUE. LOVE, LEE
LOZANO!! [WALTER REPLIES BY LETTER BEFORE HE LEAVES TOWN FOR SUMMER. JULY 5]

/ " 23 — FELIX ROTH COMES FOR A "DIALOGUE", LAYING ON ME ALL THE
PROBLEMS OF THE MIDDLE CLASS INCLUDING OPERATIONS.

/ " 24 — JAKE (NEIGHBOR, 2 LOFT BLDGS EAST OF MINE) UNEXPECTEDLY DROPS
IN THRU FIRE ESCAPE DOOR WHICH I OPEN IN HOT WEATHER.
WE HAVE DIALOGUE INCLUDING STOCK MARKET INFO & DRUG
INFO.

// " 30 — I RECEIVE A VISIT FROM ROMY McDONALD & HER FRIEND
MARGO WHO WERE GIVEN MY NAME IN ENGLAND BY
TIM HEAD. PASS INFO.

/ JULY 9, 69 — JASON CRUM COMES & IS INTERESTING BUT WE DO NOT
HAVE DIALOGUE.

/ " 9, 69 — ARTHUR BERMAN COMES & IS NOT VERY INTERESTING
BUT WE DO NOT HAVE DIALOGUE. (SEE JULY 17)

/ " 10 — KASS ZAPKUS & I HAVE TERRIFIC DIALOGUE, MUCH ABT THE
ART WORKERS COALITION, BUT THEN OUR DIALOGUES HAVE
ALWAYS BEEN GOOD & ARE MELLOW BY NOW.

/ " 11 — START DIALOGUE WITH HUGO THE CAT, WHO WILL LIVE
HERE FOR A WHILE WHILE HIS OWNERS (██ NEIGHBORS
BILL & CHARLOTTE SAYLER) ARE OUT OF TOWN. HE MAULS MY
ARM AS A START BUT THE DIALOGUE PROGRESSES SLIGHTLY TO A
GOOD FIGHTING DIALOGUE. ONE WKEND IS ALL I CAN TAKE WITH HUGO.

/ " 15 — BOB HUOT COMES. WE HAVE RATHER STIFF FORMAL EXCHANGE.
I TRY AN ABRUPT MOVE TO WAKE HIM UP.

/ " 16 — BOB (SMITTY) SMITHSON ARRIVES EARLY. IT IS A MATTER
OF DISCOMFORT I THINK. BUT I GET A LOT OF INFO OUT.
(HE WANTS MY INFO).

/ " 17 — ARTHUR BERMAN BRINGS DOC HUGHES. DOC DOES HIS RAPP &
THEN GOES TO SLEEP. HAVE BETTER TALK WITH ARTHUR.

// " 24 — RECEIVE A VISIT FROM PHYLLIS ROSEN & PORTIA HARCUS, WHO
HAVE GALLERIES IN BOSTON. WE TALK ALOT & I LEARN ALOT.
IT WAS A GOOD DIALOGUE (TRIALOGUE). ABT 3 HRS, MAYBE MORE.

/ " 26 — WESTON NAEF HAS HIS OWN INFO BUT ALSO ALLOWS HIMSELF
TO BE DRENCHED BY MY INFO. 4 HRS.

/ " 28 — MARCIA TUCKER STAYS 3 HRS, ASKS GOOD QUESTIONS, INTENSE
IF SOMEWHAT GOSSIPISH DIALOGUE, BUT SHE ENJOYS THE PLAY OF
DIALOGUE MEANING.

/ AUG 1, 69 — MIKE SHORE & I WERE FALLING ASLEEP FROM BOREDOM WITH "CONVERSATION"
SO I SUGGESTED WE GO OUT & WE RAN AROUND DOING ERRANDS &
STOPPING IN STORES, ESPECIALLY THE BICYCLE STORE IN E. VILLAGE.

/ AUG 8, 69 — KENT CLINOW. TOLD A GREAT "HOW I GOT MY 1Y RATING" STORY.

/ AUG 19, 69 — JIM HARITHAS IS AS MODERN & INTERESTING AS EVER — WE HAVE
VERY GOOD DIALOGUE. INFO FROM THE WORLD OF MUSEUMS, TRUSTEES &
"POLITICAL HEAVIES." (CONTINUED ON P. 44A)

Dialogue Piece (part four), 1969. Ink on paper, 11 × 8½ in. (27.9 × 21.6 cm)

<u>DIALOGUE PIECE</u> (CONTINUED) (p.43A)

AUG 26, 69 – LARRY STAFFORD RET'NS.

SEPT 2 – DAVID LEE RET'NS. ▬ CONTRAST WITH HIS VISIT MAY 20, 69.

SEPT 10 – JERRY KNASTER COMES TO PICK UP DOPE. THIS VISIT WAS SLIGHTLY BETTER THAN LAST TIME HE CAME TO SEE ME.

SEPT 10 – TED CASTLE. FOR SOME REASON, I NO LONGER GET TURNED ON BY HIS IDEAS, BUT HE WASN'T RELAXED.

SEPT 11 – DAVID LEVIN, FAGGOT, EX-ANDOVER, STAYS 6 HRS, HONEST TALK.

SEPT. 19 – JILLEN LOWE COMES TO SEE WK (SHE'S A DOUBLE LEO).

SEPT. 20 – TED CASTLE RET'NS ONCE MORE FOR A BRIEF VISIT.

SEPT. 21 – JAMES LEE BYARS STRETCHES OUT ON BED FOR ENTIRE DIALOGUE ENJOYING WINDOW VIEW, BOURBON, GRASS, ETC.

SEPT. 22 – JILLEN LOWE RET'NS BRINGING BARON & BARONESS JOHN & HELEN VON ECHT (BOTH RICH, YOUNG, BEAUTIFUL & A LOT OF FUN). FOR A CHANGE A PLEASURABLE EXCHANGE WITH COLLECTORS.

SEPT 29 – JILLEN LOWE BRINGS JEFF PALEY. THIS WAS MORE OF A TRILOGUE. JEFF PALEY WAS MORE INTEREST(ED) THAN (ING).

OCT 1 – CLEMENT MEADMORE BRINGS THE ▬ ENGLISH WOMAN JENNIFER A. TOWNDROW FOR A BRIEF, PACKED DIALOGUE BETW. THEM & MY WORK. SHE'S WITH <u>STUDIO VISTA</u> PUBL., LONDON.

OCT 1 – KEITH SONNIER & I ON SOME PREVIOUS VISITS HE MADE ▬ HERE HAD MORE FUN TALKING THAN WE DID TODAY, BUT IT WAS OKAY.

OCT 8 – BILLY BRYANT COPLEY & I HAD AS GOOD A DIALOGUE TODAY AS ANY PREVIOUSLY & WE DIDN'T EVEN TURN ON TILL THE END.

OCT 12 – MILES FORST HASN'T BEEN HERE FOR A LONG TIME BUT UNFORTUNATELY I WAS TOO TIRED TO BE ENTHUSIASTIC.

OCT 14 – GREGOIRE MÜLLER & WHEE KIM COME UNANNOUNCED (FROM PARIS) ▬ GIVEN MY NAME BY BELLAMY. DAN GRAHAM HAPPENED TO BE HERE & HE & I BOTH DUMPED OUR OWN INFO ON THEM. GREGOIRE SAYS I AM THE ONLY ▬ ENTHUSIASTIC ABT N.Y.C.

OCT 16 – MAX HUTCHINSON FROM AUSTRALIA INVITES ME TO JOIN GALLERY HE'S OPENING HERE BUT I TELL HIM AT PRESENT I DON'T WANT TO JOIN ANY GALLERY. DIALOGUE MOSTLY ABOUT GALLERIES. JOLLY MAX.

OCT 16 – MILES FORST & I HAVE A MUCH BETTER TALK, ▬ A LOT ABOUT TEACHING.

OCT 22 – HAVE ONE OF THE BEST DIALOGUES I'VE HAD IN A LONG TIME: MURRAY HOCHMAN.

Dialogue Piece (part five), 1969. Ink on paper, 11 × 8½ in. (27.9 × 21.6 cm)

<u>DIALOGUE PIECE</u> (CONT.) (P. 44A)

OCT 27, 69 – MAC DODY (FROM WHITNEY MUS.) ~~STRUCK OUT~~ DOESN'T
    GET TURNED ON BY ABSTRACT PAINTINGS BUT SURE
    DIGS ON MY COMIX. ~~STRUCK OUT~~ THAT'S ALL RIGHT.
    BELTS TWO BOURBONS FOR HIS TRIP TO THE
    SUBURBS.

NOV 1, 69 – LARRY STAFFORD RETNS & WE ARE BOTH MORE
    RELAXED & HAVE MORE FUN.

NOV 7, 69 – ROLF RICKE BRINGS FRIEND HANS, FROM GERMANY,

NOV 8 – AMANDA (MACKIE?) FROM WHEATON COLLEGE VISITS
    AS A RESULT OF THE COLLOQUIUM THERE ON NOV 6.
    SHE IS BRIGHT & SOPHISTICATED, PRETTY, FAMILY LIVES
    IN N.Y.C. (16TH & AVE A?). WE HAVE VERY GOOD TALK
    ESPECIALLY TOWARDS END. SHE HAS HER OWN GRASS
    & WE GET SMASHED ON IT. HER (MALE) FAMILY PICKS
    HER UP (HER MOTHER CALLS WHEN SHE IS HERE).

NOV 10 – ALAN BAYMAN (BAIMAN?) WHO WAS SENT BY JILLEN
    LOWE IS VERY DRAGGY, FROM BROOKLYN (BUT
    NOT JEWISH, BUT I NEVER KNOW WHO IS & WHO
    ISN'T).

NOV 11 – CONNIE BOWER VISITS TO PICK DRAWINGS FOR
    "ART RESOURCES CENTER OF THE WHITNEY MUSEUM
    OF AMERICAN ART" (NOV 22 – DEC 6, 185 CHERRY ST.
    NEAR MANHATTAN BRIDGE & SOUTH ST).

NOV 11 – BRIEF DIALOGUE WITH JERRY "WALKER" TO WHOM
    I GIVE SOME ACID (INSTEAD OF ASS, AS KALTEN-
    BACH SAID). PICK-UP FROM ST. ADRIAN'S.

NOV 16 – KASS-KES ZAPKUS BRINGS OVER MR & MRS FRANKEL,
    THE FRANKELS, FROM CHICAGO, TO TURN THEM ON. THEY GET
    HIGH JUST FINE, OFFER ME <u>MONEY</u> WHICH
    I REFUSE TELLING THEM I'M INSULTED THAT
    THEY OFFERED, & WE PART SUGARLY.

NOV 17 – CINDY NEMSER. ARIES. I LIKE ~~STRUCK~~ ARIES ~~STRUCK~~
    WOMEN, THEY'RE NOT SENTIMENTAL. THE BIG
    BROOKLYN REBELLION.

NOV 18 – LARRY FRIFELD (SP.?) DROPS IN, <u>GOOD</u> <u>TALK</u>.

NOV 19 – GEORGE ("DICK") BELLAMY COMES AGAIN, SLIGHTLY
    LESS HARD WORK, THAN LAST TIME HE WAS HERE ENIGMA AT END (BOTH VERY HIGH),
    INSCRUTABLE AS SOMETIMES BEFORE,

Dialogue Piece (part six), 1969. Ink on paper, 11 × 8½ in. (27.9 × 21.6 cm)

DIALOGUE PIECE (CONT. P.45A)

NOV. 20,69 - FINALLY A GROUP DIALOGUE, GARY BOWER BRINGS KIDS FROM ART RESOURCES CENTER OF WHITNEY MUS, FOR A TERRIFIC EXPERIENCE FOR ME. ABOUT 18 KIDS. TALK MOSTLY TO A BOY* WHO'S GOING BACK TO HIS FARM IN MICH., SAID HE'S THE ONLY ONE WHO'S NOT STAYING IN N.Y.C. OF HIS GROUP. SAID MINE OF ALL THEIR SYMPOSIUMS SO FAR ■ WAS MOST "DISORDERLY," THE LEAST "STRICT."
*BILL GOERS.

NOV. 28,69 - DR & MRS. MILTON BRUTTEN FROM PHILADELPHIA. ~~~~~~~~ DR. BRUTTEN, A CHILD PSYCHOLOGIST, WANTED TO TALK ABOUT ART & I WANTED TO TALK ABT PSYCHOLOGY, WHICH SEEMS LIKE THE CONDITIONS FAVORABLE TO A GOOD DIALOGUE.

DEC 4,69 - FRED GUTZEIT & I HAVE INSTANT GOOD SCORPIO COMMUNICATION.

DEC 5,69 - AGNES DENES TELLS ME ABT DIALECTIC TRIANGULATION, HER DO-IT-YRSELF PHILOSOPHY.

DEC 5,69 - ERIC, A STUDENT, COMES BY WITH KALTENBACH & THE DIALOGUE IS ~~~~~~ MOSTLY NON-VERBAL.

DEC 8,69 - ED SHOSTAK, AN OLD FRIEND, GIVES A VERY GENEROUS & HIGH-INFO DIALOGUE WHICH I ENJOYED.

DEC 12,69 - GARY BOWER RETN'S FOR A 7-HR DIALOGUE THIS TIME. I THANK HIM FOR LETTING ME GET OUT SO MANY IDEAS.

DEC 13,69 - LEFTY (SEBASTIAN) ADLER & I WERE JUST GETTING INTO A DIALOGUE WHEN BOB STANLEY WHO BROUGHT HIM DRAGS HIM AWAY.

DEC 18,69 - DINE AT ED & CINDY FELDMAN'S WHERE THE MOST EXQUISITE DIALOGUE TAKES PLACE.

Dialogue Piece (part seven), 1969. Ink on paper, 11 × 8½ in. (27.9 × 21.6 cm)

Peers

Dialogue Piece was meant to take place with a diverse range of people, including Lozano's mother, a cat, and a baby, and, most importantly, key members of the New York scene at the time: Walter De Maria, Jasper Johns, John Giorno, and Yvonne Rainer being among the first she invited. Lozano's engagement and satisfaction with this work ("What if I stopped doing different <u>pieces</u> & just did the <u>dialogue piece</u> for the rest of my life as my 'work'?") suggest how her discomfort with the art scene might not have been directed so much at the *who* and *what* but rather at the *where* and *how* it was taking place. On the following pages, an annotated list of select participants in *Dialogue Piece* maps Lozano's social network, a microcosm of the New York art at the end of the 1960s.

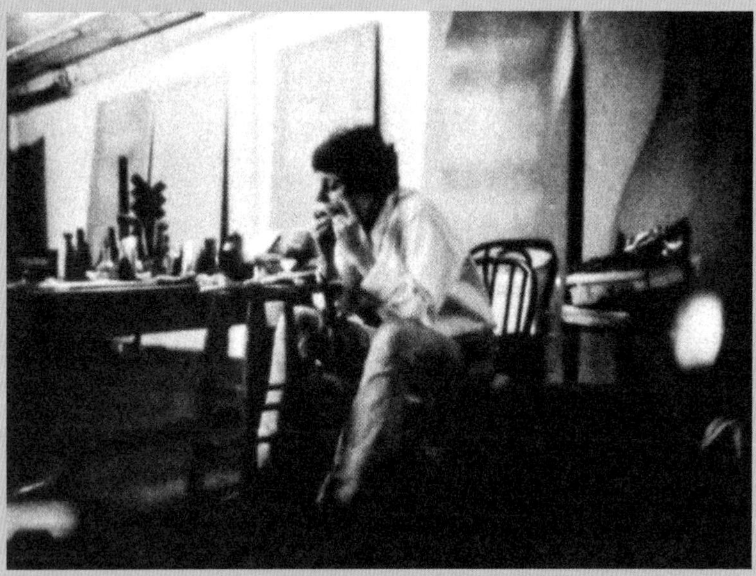

Lozano in her Grand Street studio where she hosted *Dialogue Piece*, ca. 1969

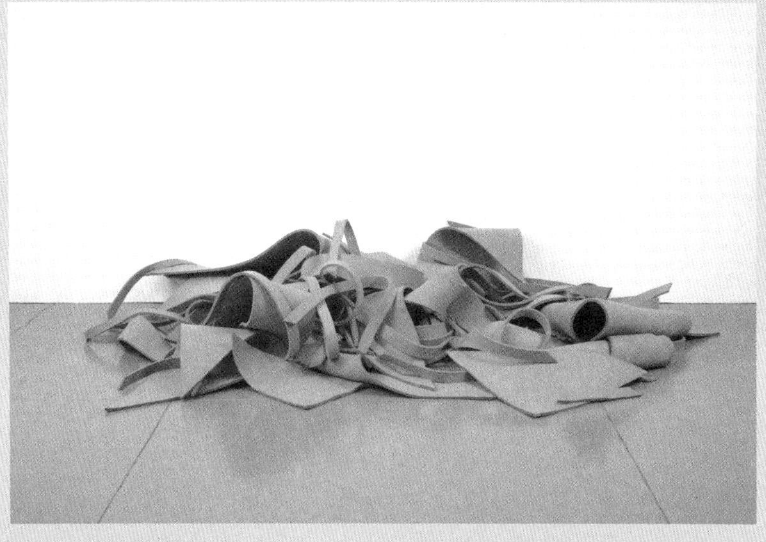

Robert Morris, *Untitled (Pink Felt)*, 1970. Felt, dimensions variable

Robert Morris (1931–2018)—nicknamed "Moose" by Lozano—was a leading figure in Minimalism in the early 1960s, but by 1968, he had abandoned its rigid materials and strict geometry to work with softer, organic materials like felt. His ideas were articulated in his seminal 1968 *Artforum* article "Anti Form," which advocated for an emphasis on process and material. Morris's ideas helped usher in the sculptural movement known as Post-Minimalism, associated with artists such as Eva Hesse and Richard Serra (who also participated in a dialogue with Lozano). Lozano's notebooks include frequent critiques of Morris's work and ideas. *Dialogue Piece* commenced on April 21, 1969, with a call to Morris.

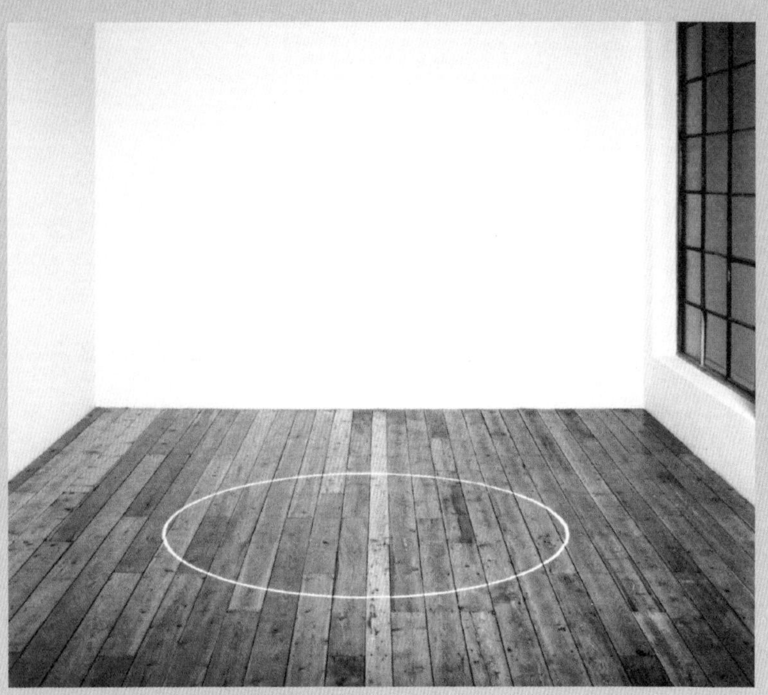

Ian Wilson, *Circle on the Floor (Chalk Circle)*, 1968. Chalk, 70 × 70 in. (178 × 178 cm)

Ian Wilson (1940–2020) was a pioneering Conceptual artist who was firmly committed to the dematerialization of art. In 1968 he made his last physical work, *Circle on the Floor (Chalk Circle)*—a circle with a six-foot diameter drawn directly on the floor, which also included instructions for future reproductions. Later that year he began *Discussions* (1968–2008), a series of conversations he hosted about art. Neither recorded nor transcribed, this conceptual project shares concerns with *Dialogue Piece*.

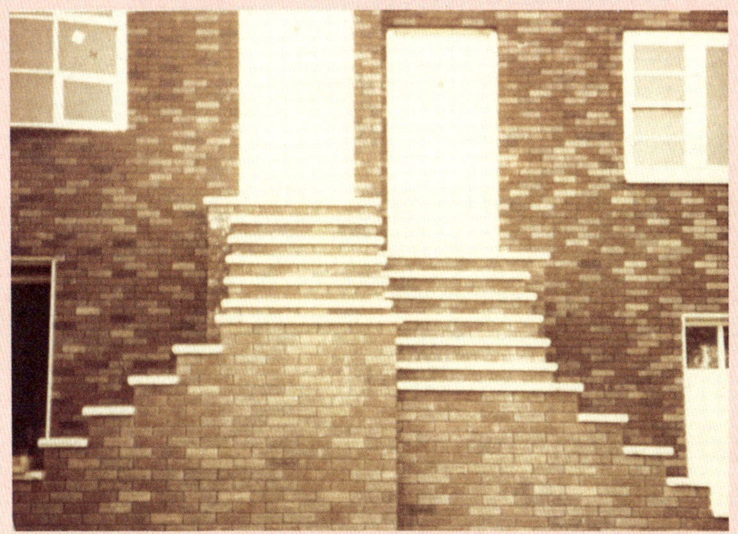

Dan Graham, *Ground-Level, Two Home Home, Jersey City, N.J.*, 1966. Chromogenic print, 2½ × 3⁹⁄₁₆ in. (6.3 × 8.9 cm)

Dan Graham (1942–2022) was one of Lozano's closest friends and collaborators in New York. Her notebooks reveal that they were, at times, in daily contact. In his wide-ranging practice—including writing, performance, architectural installation, and video—Graham sought to question the relationship between viewer and object and public and private. His seminal work, *Homes for America* (1966–67), presents photographs of suburban houses in a grid-like layout, slyly equating the serial repetition of Minimalist sculpture with postwar housing development. The work was originally developed as a magazine piece rather than for display in a gallery. In 1970, Graham included write-ups of Lozano's *Grass Piece* and *No-Grass Piece* in his short-lived magazine *End Moments*.

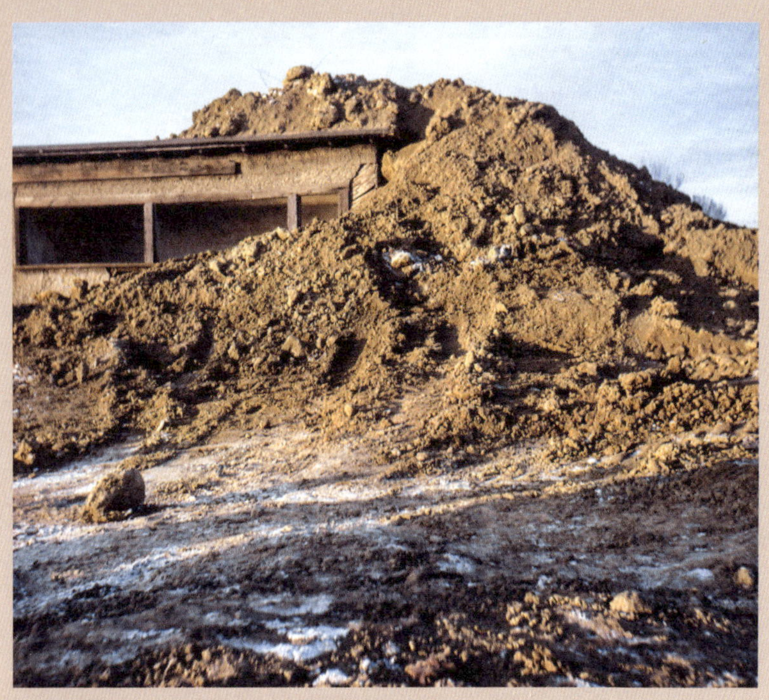

Robert Smithson, *Partially Buried Woodshed*, 1970. Woodshed and twenty truckloads of earth, 18 × 10 × 45 ft. (5.5 × 3 × 13.7 m)

Robert Smithson (1938–1973) began making Minimalist sculpture in the early 1960s. As the decade went on, he became increasingly concerned with the gallery system and art's context. In 1968 he exhibited a series titled *Site/Nonsite*, sculptural containers that held natural elements, such as dirt, sand, and rocks. These works anticipated his seminal earthworks: large-scale outdoor sculptures and installations comprising materials from the surrounding landscape. Writing about their dialogue, Lozano observed: "SMITHSON DIALOGUE SMITTY LIKES MY IDEA OF INVESTIGATIONS BUT WOULD EVEN PREFER INQUISITIONS."

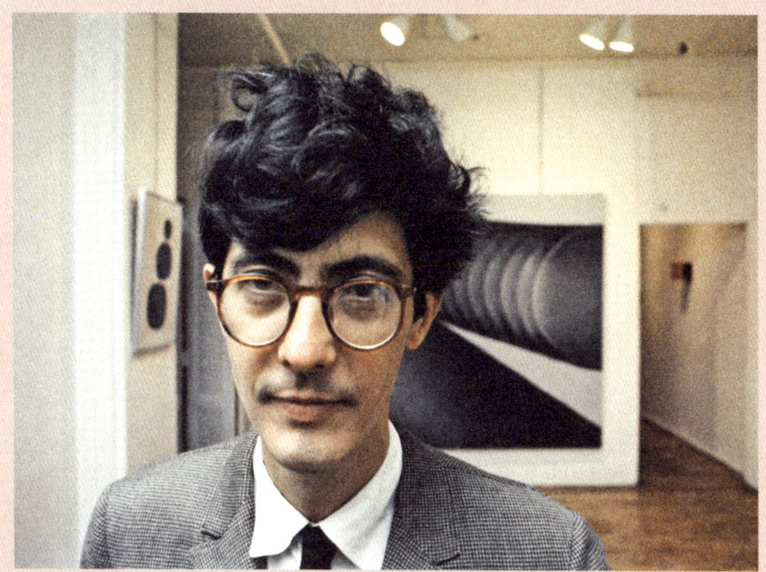

Bellamy at the Green Gallery with Lozano's painting *Veer* (1964) on view behind him, 1964

Richard "Dick" Bellamy (1927–1998) was the founder and director of the influential Green Gallery from 1960 to 1965, and later director at the Noah Goldowsky Gallery. As a dealer, he championed the career of leading Pop, Minimal, and Conceptual artists, including Dan Flavin, Donald Judd, Walter De Maria, Robert Morris, Claes Oldenburg, James Rosenquist, and Richard Serra, among others. He was influential in Lozano's career in New York, including her work in several exhibitions at the Green Gallery.

1ST WK AUGUST, 71

DECIDE TO BOYCOTT WOMEN.
THROW LUCY LIPPARD'S ~~SECOND~~ 2ND LETTER ON DEFUNCT PILE, UNANSWERED.
DO NOT GREET ROCHELLE BASS IN STORE.

2ND WK AUGUST, 71

PAULA TAVINS CALLS AUG 11. TELL HER I AM BOYCOTTING WOMEN
AS AN EXPERIMENT THRU ABT SEPT & THAT AFTER THAT
"COMMUNICATION WILL BE BETTER THAN EVER."

PEYOTE TRIP AUG 10 71 : PURIFICATION
OF THE UNCONSCIOUS*. I BEAT THE SAND WITH JAKE'S
PUSSYWILLOW WHIP.
                                        * DEEPBRAIN
I STOP HOLDING ON TO WALTER DE MARIA.

AUG 12 71
IM FUCKIN UP BAD, MAKIN MISTAKES. ONE HOUR LATE TO MEET
BELLAMY HERE, I MISSED HIM (HE LEAVES NOTE) IT'S MY DEEPBRAIN
RESISTANCE TO ... WHAT? BELLAMY? KELSEY? DO I WANT TO LOSE
MY LOFT FOR ACTION? UTTER CLAUSTROPHOBIA IN TIME/SPACE OF PRESENT.
I MISSED HIM ALL LAST WEEK TOO.

ALSO FUCKED UP WITH BUSINESS COMPATIBILITY BOOK.

EXPERIMENT: WRITE TO PEOPLE IN ATTEMPT TO
COMMUNICATE AFTER MERCURY GOES RETROGRADE AUG 13.
TRY SOME LOCAL VISITS.

GOING ▄▄ TO ROOF LOOKING UP AT MARS & (STRAIGHT) QUARTER
MOON, STARS & DOWN ON NEIGHBOORHOOD CALMS ▄▄ ▄▄▄ ME.

FROM WEEK IN HALIFAX : THE MAGIC WORD TO CANCEL SPELLS
IF ANYONE TRIES TO LAY A SPELL ON YOU, OR, TO COUNTERACT A
WITCH'S POWER; YELL: ORTHOGRAPHY!

No title, 1971. Ink on paper, 9⅛ × 8½ in. (23.3 × 21.5 cm)

Boycott Women

It had happened in the past that Lozano dramatically proclaimed her intention to take—or abstain from—a substance, an action, or even a person, only to ultimately disregard her own proposal. This time, however, something ruptured differently. Following her exhibition at the Whitney Museum, events derailed, taking an irreversible turn that led to the final work within her destructionist series: *Boycott Women*. When considered in tandem with *Dropout Piece*, this boycott seems to pave the way to the definitive execution of Lozano's self-exile.

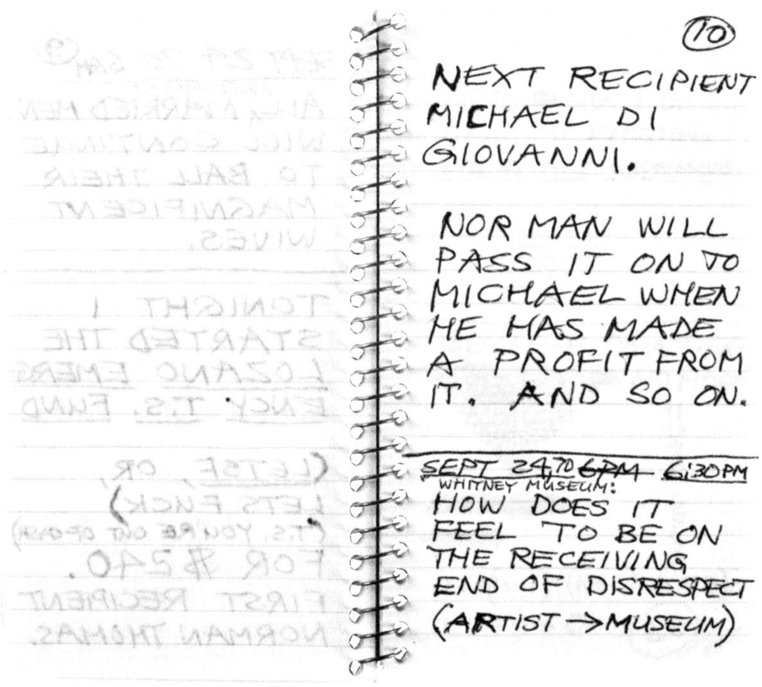

Private Book 2, September 24, 1970, p. 10

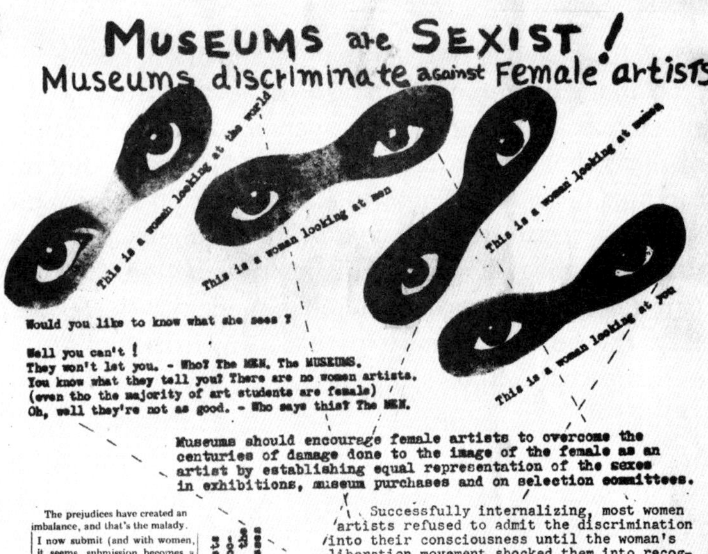

Women Artists in Revolution flyer, ca. 1970

In fall 1970, while Lozano was preparing for her opening
at the museum, a public confrontation was unfolding
in parallel, regarding a show scheduled to open just ten
days after hers—the Whitney Sculpture Biennial. The Ad
Hoc Women Artists Committee—born of the Art Workers'
Coalition under the initiative of, among others, Poppy
Johnson, Faith Ringgold, and Lucy Lippard—together with
Women Artists in Revolution, and Women Students and
Artists for Black Artists' Liberation, targeted the museum
for the lack of women in the biennial. The group staged
weekly protests outside of the museum, demanding that
50 percent of the artists in the upcoming exhibition be
women, with the additional request that half of these
women be Black (in the end, 22 of the 103 artists included
were women). One of the entries recorded in Lozano's
notebooks, dated September 24, 1970, hints at a certain
affinity with the protesting groups: "Whitney Museum:
How does it feel to be on the receiving end of disrespect
(artist → museum)." Yet, when she took part in one of the
preparatory meetings before the protests, in November
1970, she dismissed it as "the same jibberjabber allcunt
disorder as in juniorhighschool girlsclub days" (p. 133).

The Whitney responded to the attacks, and among its
defenses it highlighted how, in recent years, the museum
had given solo shows to several women, the most recent
in the list being Lozano. We can guess how furious she
must have been when she read the statement. Not only
was she being reduced to the identity of "woman"—a
categorization she had been actively resisting since first
rejecting it at the age of fourteen—but this flattening was
also being employed to protect an institution she despised
and a position she didn't respect. Furthermore, her work,
created with the ambition to instigate revolution, was being

reduced to something merely suitable for exhibition to fulfill a quota, thus feeding precisely into the reactionary, reformist system she sought to dismantle. After the closing of her Whitney exhibition, she bluntly wrote, "Women's lib brought bad luck."

In August 1971, seven months after her Whitney exhibition closed, Lozano finally decided to "boycott women"—including herself, one could argue. The Whitney Museum events might have been the final straw, as we know that she started her boycott by leaving a letter from Lucy Lippard unanswered. Twice. The piece was supposed to last only a few months, yet records show that she actively avoided unnecessary exchanges with women for the rest of her life.

Although Lozano's fight against the constructed concept of womanhood is well known, it remains debatable why, from that moment on, not talking to members of her own gender was the only solution she envisioned. What is clear is that, in 1960s society, the only way to truly have agency was to be a (white, cis) man—a truth that had persisted for centuries and, to varying degrees, continues today. For many artists who did not fit this mold, the only available strategy was to assimilate, thereby getting as close as possible to the conventional man. Lozano mastered this trick. But, as the feminist movement started charting a new vision of womanhood, she was forced to confront the limits of her own position: she was not one of the guys, and she certainly did not want to be one of the girls—yet she had already been assigned a category. There was no longer a space in which Lozano could operate within masculinity, or a viable position outside of femininity. Within this binary framework, engaging with other women would have meant being caught in the act, being infected by the disease of

Life and Work

femaleness, and ultimately proving the institution right: indeed, she also was a woman. Lozano found herself at a dead end. It became evident that the only form of control she could exert was not over which subject she could claim to be, but rather over the choice of being a subject at all. Her only true agency lay in orchestrating her own disappearance.

PAST: "MEN FIGHT EACH OTHER, WOMEN BORE EACH OTHER"

TWO WOMEN CALLED TO TELL ME ABOUT THE MEETING AT WHICH WHITE & BLACK FEMALE ARTISTS WOULD DISCUSS DEMANDING 50% FEMALE REPRESENTATION IN THE WHITNEY SCULPTURE ANNUAL. I THOUGHT I'D BETTER NOT COPOUT. WHEN I GOT THERE IT WAS THE SAME JIBBERJABBER ALLCUNT DISORDER AS IN JUNIORHIGHSCHOOL GIRLSCLUB DAYS. A SELFAPPOINTED CHAIRWOMAN COULD NOT CONTROL THE BLABNOISE. I SMOKED GRASS THROUGHOUT LIKE I DO WHEN I'M HOME. A NICE BLACK SISTER TRAPPED ME IN THE TYPICAL POWERGAME, IT WAS PLAYED OVER AN ASHTRAY. LATER TWO ▬▬▬ WOMEN PATTED ME ON THE HEAD. I OFFERED A TASTE OF GRASS TO TWO OTHER NICE BLACK SISTERS BUT THEY SAID NO. SOME HEAVIES SPOKE WITH AFFECTED INFLECTIONS. I STRONGLY FELT THE PRESENCE OF LOTSA MEN AT THE MEETING.

↑
EARLY NOV, 70 – MEETING AT LUCY LIPPARD'S.

WOMEN'S LIB BROUGHT BAD LUCK. (FEB, 71)

Women's Lib Brought Bad Luck, 1971. Ink on vellum paper, 7 × 8½ in. (18 × 22 cm)

54A.
ONE YEAR'S ~~SALARY~~ WAGES
OF THE ~~ONE~~ PERSON
(OR AVERAGE YEARLY ~~PAY~~
WAGES IF MORE THAN
ONE PERSON) WHO CLEANS
THE TOILET & CONNECTED
LOUNGE AREAS & IN THE
MUSEUM, PUBLIC & ~~PRIVATE~~
~~THE~~ MUSEUM STAFF,
DEALERS:

MAY 22   54.
NATURAL
PLAN YR ∧ DEATH
FOR YR BIRTHDAY
(NOV. 5) IN THE YEAR
2001. THAT'LL
MAKE ME 71 WHEN
                DECIDE WHETHER TO
I ∧ DIE, JUST ABOUT
RIGHT, & I'LL LIVE
TO "SEE" THE 21ST
CENTURY (WHICH I
ALWAYS HOPED I
WOULD), OF COURSE
THIS COMMEMORATES
A GREAT FILM WHICH
MOVED ME VERY
MUCH (FIRST TIME I
SAW IT WAS THE 3
HAPPIEST HOURS OF
MY LIFE, I SAY SMIL-
             DECIDING ABOUT
ING) AND ∧ DYING ON
MY BIRTHDAY IS

                 MOST   55.
~~NEVER~~ THE ∧ FINAL
STATEMENT A
SCORPIO CAN MAKE
(BY THEN I'LL HAVE
EARNED MY EAGLE
WINGS & PERHAPS
        MIGHT
~~COULD~~ MAKE IT TO
"PHOENIX").
DOVE, ~~OR~~ BLACK PANTHER.

I TAKE POSSESSION
OF MARION'S BOX!

IT HOLDS MY STAMPS
PERFECTLY, SNUGLY,
HAPPILY.

THE TAKE POSSESSION
PIECE COULD DEVELOP
INTO SOMETHING
INTERESTING?

Private Book 2, 1969, pp. 54A–55

Plan Your Natural Death

The fantasy of planning her own death was present in Lozano's thoughts. In a notebook she scheduled her natural death for November 5, 2001—her seventy-first birthday. She felt that the timing was "just about right," and would give her the chance to "see" the twenty-first century, which she "always hoped" she would. The paradox of planning a "natural" death perfectly embodied Lozano's fixation on control—her urgent need to feel fiercely independent, even from death. But it was also a direct consequence of her philosophical vision of existence. Both her scientific and esoteric perspectives pointed to a coherent underlying system governing reality, in which chance and necessity collided—this was evidenced, for instance, by the "'striking' structural similarity between the I Ching and the subatomic theory of quarks," or by the sharp astrological observations that punctuated her notebooks.

To what extent this self-narration was intentional remains unknown, but by 1971, her artistic practice, her thought process, and the conditions of her life had aligned in an almost fateful way: her *Boycott Women* coincided with the end of her career (as we know it), just as her decision to leave coincided with an eviction notice from her studio due to unpaid rent. In a kind of self-fulfilling prophecy, *Dropout Piece* had, indeed, become inevitable. A few weeks into her boycott, Lozano seemed to reach her point of non-return. She wrote: "I have no identity. I have an approximate mathematical identity (birthchart). I have several names. I will give up my search for identity as a deadend investigation. I will make myself empty to receive cosmic info" (p. 137).

Lozano's process of self-emptying from her own identity in order to receive "cosmic info" was consistent with her earlier attempt to limit her consumption in *Dropout*. In her habit-dismantling project, she had reached the core of the question, the production and consumption of her very self. In order for *Dropout* to work, she had to leave her artistic persona: "I <u>will</u> renounce the artist's ego . . . I <u>will</u> be human first, artist second." The process was paralleled by the corresponding evacuation of her studio and the severing of most of her relationships—at least, the remaining ones, since women were already out of the picture. Finally, her spoliation included her name, which she abandoned in favor of other options until she finally settled on the vowel "E," leaving the vestiges of her old identity to turn into pure energy.

Despite her disappearance plans, E spent another decade in New York, moving from one couch to the next until she found herself gravitating around the younger punk scene. Although she did consider some of her ongoing activities art, none of it was meant for the public. In 1982 she moved to Dallas, where her parents lived, and spent the remainder of her life there. Her time in Texas was marked by indigence, evictions, a restraining order from her father, and a brief stint in the hospital for treatment of cervical cancer, which ultimately killed her on October 2, 1999—two years and one month earlier than she had planned.

SEPT 8, 71

I HAVE NO IDENTITY.

I HAVE AN APPROXIMATE MATHEMATICAL IDENTITY (BIRTHCHART.)

I HAVE SEVERAL NAMES.‡

I WILL GIVE UP MY SEARCH FOR IDENTITY ~~XXXXX~~ AS A DEADEND INVESTI-GATION~~X~~.

I WILL MAKE MYSELF EMPTY ~~XX~~ TO RECIEVE COSMIC INFO.

I WILL RENOUNCE THE ARTIST'S EGO, THE SUPREME TEST WITHOUT WHICH BATTLE A HUMAN COULD NOT ~~XXXXX~~ BECOME "OF KNOWLEGE."

I WILL BE HUMAN FIRST, ARTIST SECOND.

I WILL NOT SEEK FAME, ~~XXXX~~ PUBLICITY, ~~XXXXX~~ OR SUCKCESS.

IDENTITY CHANGES CONTINUOUSLY AS MULTIPLIED BY TIME. (IDENTITY IS A VECTOR.)

‡ ON ROOF AFTER ~~XXXX~~ I WRITE THIS, CINDY TELLS ME THAT "LOZANO (THE NAME) SNAPPED OFF."

No title, 1971. Ink on vellum paper, 11 × 8½ in. (28 × 21.5 cm)

"All ends are loose ends because there are no hard edges in the universe"

In 1966, Hollis Frampton produced his third and final portrait of Lozano, this time recorded on film, as part of a series of video portraits of other friends titled *Manual of Arms* (pp. 140–41). In the black-and-white setting of a New York loft, Lozano faces the camera. Frampton films her while she thinks in silence, then she speaks, smiles, and at times bursts into unrestrained laughter. At irregular intervals, something crosses the lens, briefly and progressively obscuring the frame until it is entirely eclipsed for a few milliseconds. Lozano sinks into darkness, then emerges and disappears again, leaving us uncertain about what her shifting mood will be when the light returns. In the dimmest moments, her white teeth stand out uncannily against the darkness—a typical Lozano grin, both snarling and defiant. The montage alternates between the portrait of her tiny figure and scenes where she vanishes entirely from the frame, replaced by the towering shadow she casts on the wall.

Frampton seems to foresee how, when dealing with Lozano's legacy, looking at her presence is as important as looking at her meticulously designed absences. From her first drawings to her final act of disappearance, much of her work exists in the tension between claiming one's space and asserting one's right to strike, exerting the refusal to function under given conditions. It is precisely this interplay that leaves much of Lozano's life and intentions as uncharted territory. While she often grants us access to intimate details of her existence—sometimes disturbingly so—there is always a

　　　　　　　Life and Work

certain degree of control over what she chooses to reveal or to withhold, just as she carefully erased big chunks of her notebooks during her final edit in January 1972. The attempt at overpowering Lozano's presence with the shadows it cast was an intentional, self-inflicted act, if we consider that she decided the greatest accomplishment of her career would be not to be there at all.

The readable part of Lozano's life resembles her paintings: a small, visible fraction of a far larger, monumental shape—"a detail of a form that can be extended to infinity." The possibility of existing outside of prescribed, visible forms imbued both her work and life. "Why do you need roots when you have gravity," she asked, suggesting that traditional forms of belonging were to be discarded in order to adapt to the broader forces regulating the universe: You don't need a fixed relationship to feel anchored if there is a greater force binding us together, just as you don't need a static identity when it's energy itself that drives your existence. When we examine Lozano's uprooted, rebellious form of independence, we must resist the temptation to reduce it (exclusively) to individual rampage. It should rather be understood as part of a broader existential struggle against the human-made protocols that regulated her agency in the conservative, sexist, racist, and capitalist patriarchal society she was living in. Her actions were not mere acts of defiance, but deliberate attempts to confront these oppressive systems, reassessing them as insignificant conventions in light of deeper energies.

What Lozano "dropped out" from might now be partially clear, but what she *dove into*—or rather, what *dove into* her—is still to be searched, and the only way to do so is to follow her through a new, radical form of empirical experimentation.

Life and Work

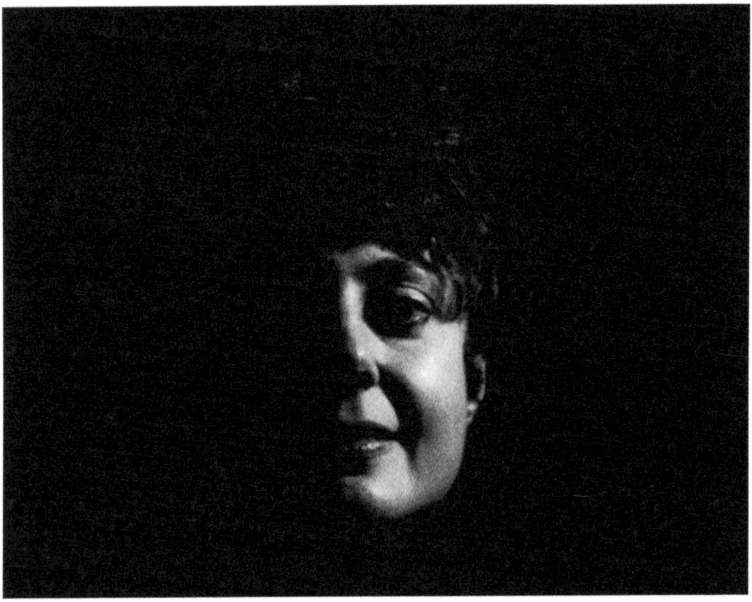

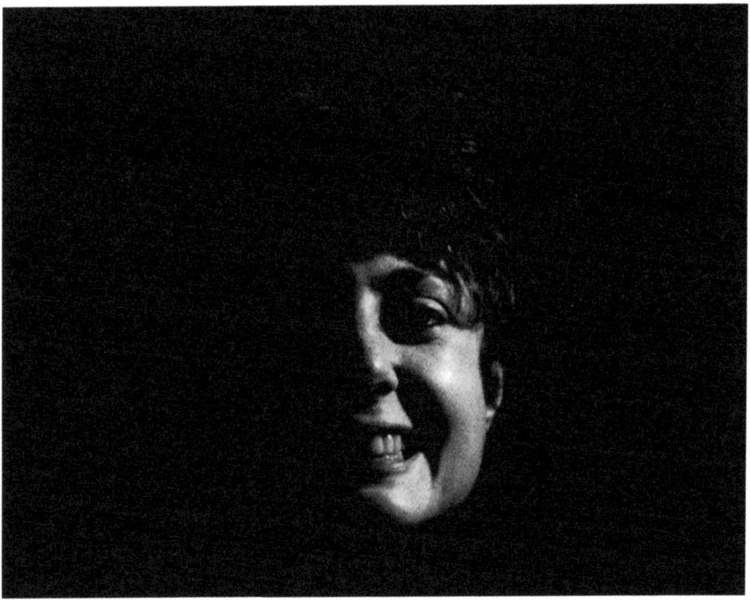

Lozano in Hollis Frampton's *Manual of Arms*, 1966

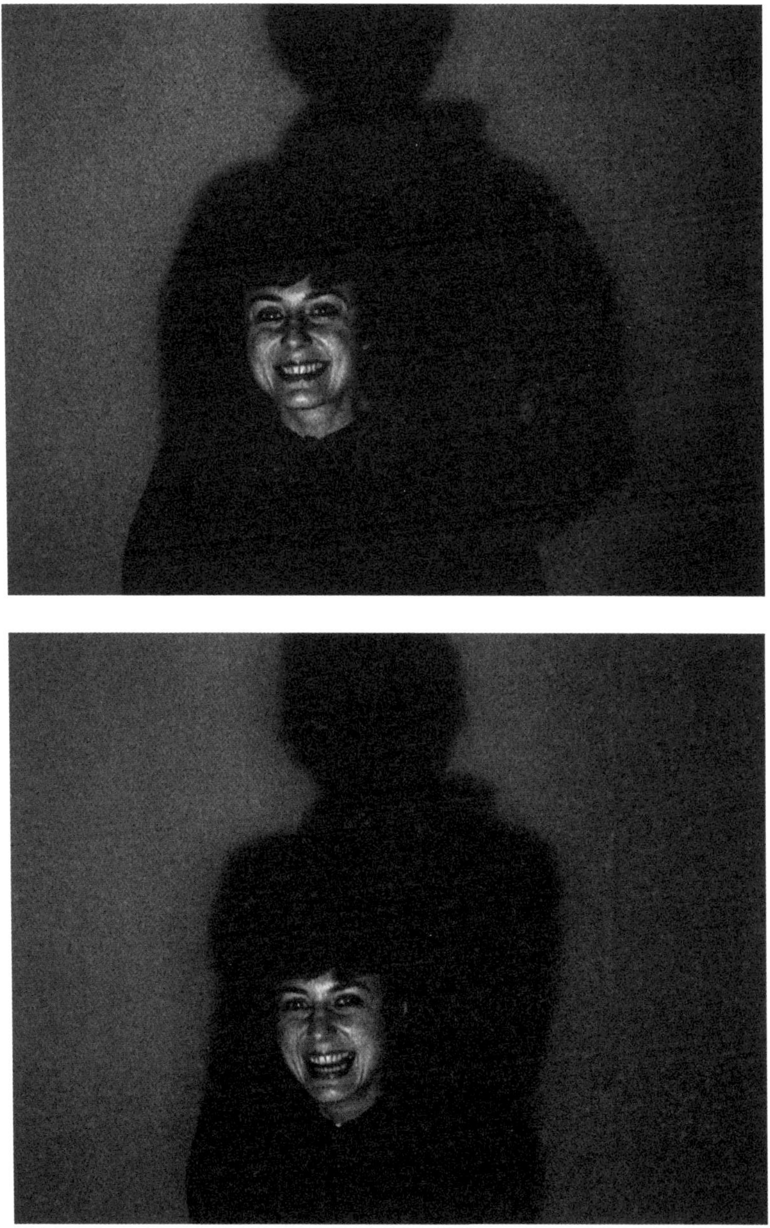

Lozano in Hollis Frampton's *Manual of Arms*, 1966

Chronology

1930 Lenore Knaster is born at 4:25 p.m. on November 5 in Newark, New Jersey. She will later proclaim the time and date of her birth her only true identity.

1944 Changes her name from Lenore to Lee as a "rejection of the traditional American middle-class female trip."

1946–51 Attends the University of Chicago, where she studies natural science and philosophy. Receives her BA in 1951.

1952–55 After graduating, begins working in the design department of the Container Corporation of America (CCA), a Chicago-based cardboard box manufacturer. The company is known for its influential use of graphic design in its products and advertisements.

At CCA she meets her future husband, the Mexican-born architect Adrian Lozano.

1956 Enrolls at the Art Institute of Chicago.

Marries Adrian Lozano in August, changing her name to Lee Lozano.

1957–59 Undergoes psychoanalysis.

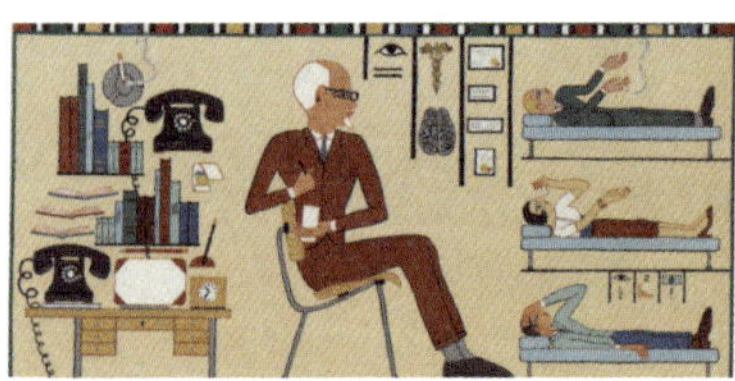

No title, n.d. Gouache, ink, and graphite on paper, 11¾ × 19⅞ in. (30 × 50.5 cm)

1960 Receives her BFA from the Art Institute of Chicago. After graduating, travels to Europe with Adrian, visiting Spain, France, and Italy. Instead of returning home to Chicago, she goes to New York alone.

She and Adrian divorce after four years of marriage. She keeps the surname Lozano.

1961 Moves to a studio at 53 West 24th Street in Manhattan.

Connects with Richard Bellamy, who is the director of the influential Green Gallery.

Through Bellamy, meets Carl Andre and Hollis Frampton.

1962 Begins making expressive, cartoonlike drawings and paintings. Images of tools, weapons, machines, airplanes, religious iconography, and aggressive, often sexual, representations of the human body frequently appear in this work. Her drawings increasingly incorporate language, often in the form of "punch line" jokes and puns.

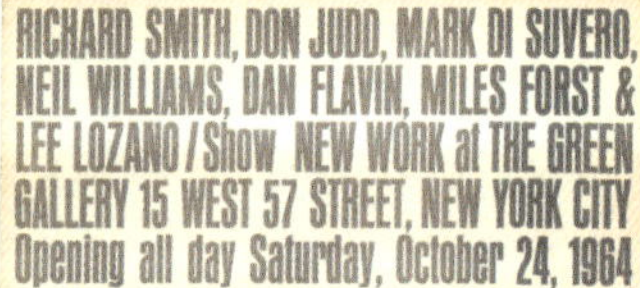

Exhibition invitation, Green Gallery, New York, 1964

1963 Begins her Tools series (1963–64), large-scale paintings and drawings of screwdrivers, clamps, wrenches, and hammers.

1964 Moves to a loft at 60 Grand Street, near Canal Street and the Bowery.

Her painterly language becomes more minimal and abstract. She develops series of large-scale paintings depicting contrasting, geometric forms, each attempting to capture the energy of an action. The titles of these works are all verbs, including *Spin* (1964), *Cram* (1965), *Swap* (1966), and *Lean* (1966).

Her paintings are included in group exhibitions at the Green Gallery.

1965 Bellamy plans her first solo exhibition for September. It is abruptly canceled when the Green Gallery closes due to financial troubles.

1966 Her solo exhibition opens on November 5, her fortieth birthday, at New York's Bianchini Gallery. She shows recent abstract paintings including *Lean*, *Clash*, and *Slide* (all 1966).

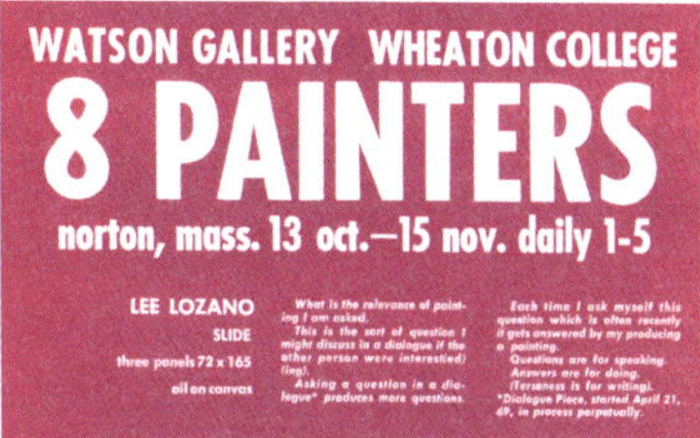

Exhibition invitation, *8 Painters*, Watson Gallery, Norton, MA, 1969

1967 Begins the *Wave* series (1967–71), a series of eleven paintings depicting the energy waves of the electromagnetic spectrum. Each painting is produced in a single session. She records information about the production of each work (time taken, drugs consumed, energy levels, etc.) in a notebook.

Starts to record her daily activities, events, and reflections in notebooks that she labels her "private notebooks." She will conceive many of these entries as conceptual "Life-Art" works (1967–70).

Meets Dan Graham toward the end of the year.

1969 On February 8, she withdraws her work from a group exhibition at Noah Goldowsky Gallery, organized by Bellamy. This action commences *General Strike Piece*, her gradual withdrawal from art-world events in pursuit of a "total personal & public revolution."

Participates in the Art Workers' Coalition (AWC) public hearing at the School of Visual Arts in New York. Nearly three hundred people attend, including Andre, Frampton, Graham, Lucy Lippard, and Hans Haacke.

Begins *Dialogue Piece*, where she invites guests to her loft for the sole purpose of having a conversation. The work officially starts on April 21, with an invitation to Robert Morris.

Exhibits *Grass Piece* and *No-Grass Piece* in *Number 7*, a group exhibition curated by Lippard at Paula Cooper Gallery. Her work is also included in *Language III* at the Dwan Gallery.

Concludes *General Strike Piece* in October by visiting exhibitions by Lynda Benglis and Sol LeWitt.

Her first European exhibition opens at Galerie Rolf Ricke in Cologne.

1970 On April 5 writes in a notebook, "It was inevitable, since I work in sets of course, that i do the Dropout (note pun) Piece. It has been churning for a long time but I think it's abt to blow."

In December, her first institutional solo exhibition opens at the Whitney Museum of American Art. The *Wave* series is exhibited alongside a group of plastic boxes containing body hair, nail clippings, and birthstones.

She ceases painting after the exhibition opens, focusing exclusively on her "Life-Art" pieces.

1971 *Infofiction*, an exhibition of her "language pieces," opens at the Nova Scotia College of Art and Design (NSCAD) in January. She exhibits

LEE LOZANO:INFOFICTION

Nova Scotia College of Art & Design
6152 Coburg Road
Halifax, Nova Scotia, Canada

January 27 - February 13, 1971

Exhibition invitation, *Infofiction*, Nova Scotia College of Art and Design, Halifax, with Lozano's handwritten note, 1971

Cash Piece, Investment Piece, Dialogue Piece, Take Possession Piece, General Strike Piece, Experience as Set Piece, Masturbation Investigation, Grass Piece, No-Grass Piece, Printed Matter Pile, and *Lozano T. S. Emergency Fund (LETSF)*. She returns in July to give a lecture about her work.

In August she writes, "Decide to boycott women. Throw Lucy Lippard's 2nd letter on defunct pile, unanswered." With this gesture, she begins her boycott of women. Conceived as a short-term experiment, she ceases communication with women for the rest of her life.

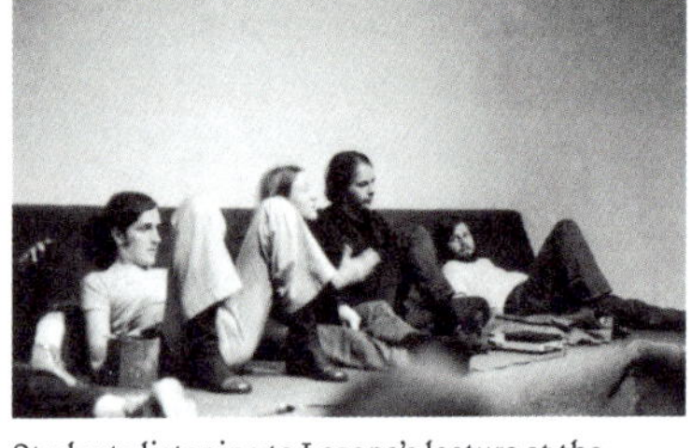

Students listening to Lozano's lecture at the Nova Scotia College of Art and Design, Halifax, July 16, 1971

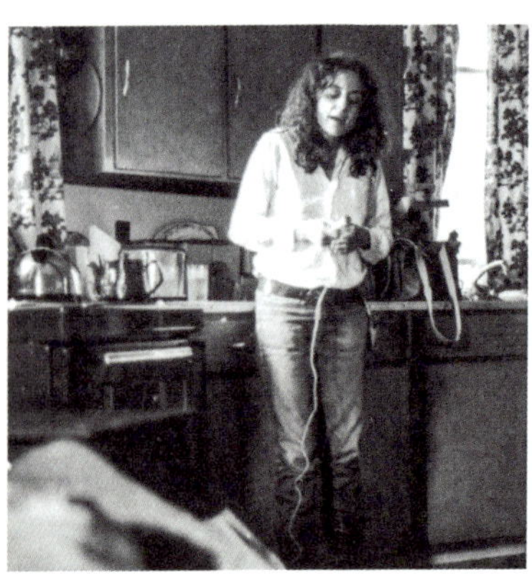

Lozano in 1971

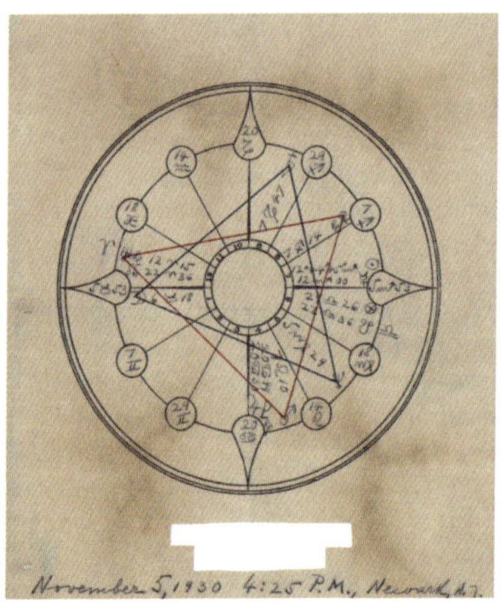

Lozano's birth chart

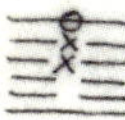

I'm Just Visiting This Planet., 1972. Ink on paper, 1½ × 4⅛ in. (3.7 × 10.5 cm)

1972 *Infofiction II* opens at Lisson Gallery in London in February. She exhibits a one-meter square of sand, placed directly on the gallery floor. Visitors are invited to write in the sand to begin a dialogue with Lozano, who is on-site during the exhibition. No one engages with the work, and the exhibition closes after just one week.

Does a sweeping edit of her eleven "private notebooks," adding, amending, and retracting certain information. She marks the date of the edit on the inside cover of each notebook.

Moves out of her Grand Street loft. Leaves her notebooks, sketchpads, and paintings with friends to ensure their safety.

Commences her *Dropout Piece*.

1973–81 Stops using the name Lee Lozano, going by Leefer and, later, Lee Free.

Little is known of her activity during these years. She no longer speaks to her friends and colleagues in the art world. She spends the remainder of the decade living in New York and traveling.

Immerses herself in a younger generation of artists, and the emerging punk scene.

1982 Moves to Dallas, Texas, where her parents live.

She now calls herself E.

Begins working with art dealers Barry Rosen and Jaap van Liere in New York, maintaining communication with them by phone.

Her work is included in the exhibition *Abstract Art of the Sixties* at the P.S.1 Institute for Art and Urban Resources (now MoMA PS1) in New York.

1998 Her work is included in four exhibitions, including *Lee Lozano / MATRIX 135* at the Wadsworth Atheneum in Hartford, Connecticut. The museum acquires the complete *Wave* series, which is included in the exhibition alongside a number of her "language pieces."

Produces her final work, *Questionnaire*, addressed to Rosen and van Liere concerning the sale of her work.

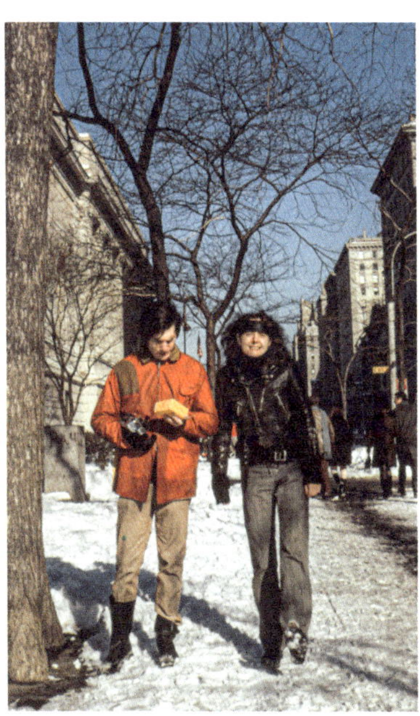

Lozano and Dan Graham, New York, early 1970s

1999 Dies on October 2 of cervical cancer, having left instructions to be buried in an unmarked grave in the Grand Prairie Memorial Gardens near Dallas.

Additional Resources

Ever since Lozano's decision to abandon the art world, historians, critics, and curators have grappled with the complexity of her life and work. Significant exhibition catalogues and monographs have examined the full breadth of Lozano's oeuvre—the evolution of her drawings and paintings, her use of language, and her multifaceted conceptual practice—assuring her place in postwar art history, while also confronting her forceful resistance to the societal and professional expectations that were placed upon her. Recent publications have reproduced her text-based language pieces and private notebooks as facsimiles, lending a materiality to her conceptual work and a powerful presence to a practice so often defined by the artist's disappearance.

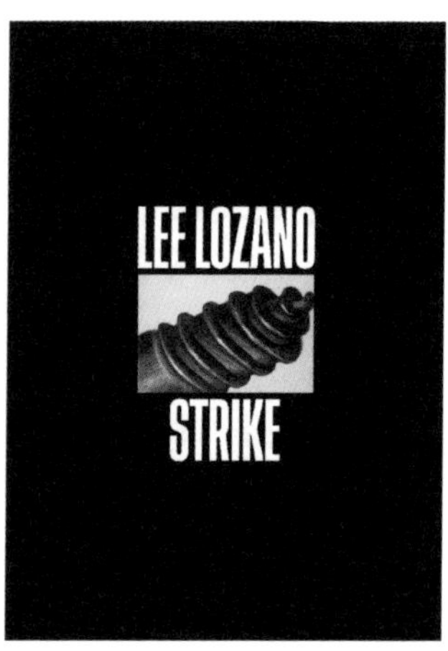

Lee Lozano: Strike (Pinacoteca Agnelli, 2023) was published on the occasion of Lozano's 2023 retrospective exhibition at Pinacoteca Agnelli, Turin, and the Bourse de Commerce, Paris. The book presents new texts by the exhibition's co-curators, Lucrezia Calabrò Visconti and Sarah Cosulich, alongside a selection of seminal writings on Lozano by Jo Applin, Lucy Lippard, and Sarah Lehrer-Graiwer, and includes a comprehensive chronology of Lozano's life.

Lee Lozano: Not Working
(Yale University Press, 2018)
is the first in-depth scholarly
monograph dedicated to Lozano's
career in New York in the 1960s.
Art historian Jo Applin traces Lozano's
wide-ranging production during this
period, culminating in her decision
to drop out of the art world. The
book offers art historical readings
of Lozano's oeuvre—placing her work
in conversation with artists including
Judith Bernstein, Mary Heilmann,
Eva Hesse, and Adrian Piper, among
others—while also presenting the
challenges Lozano's radical, defiant
practice pose to both art history
and feminism.

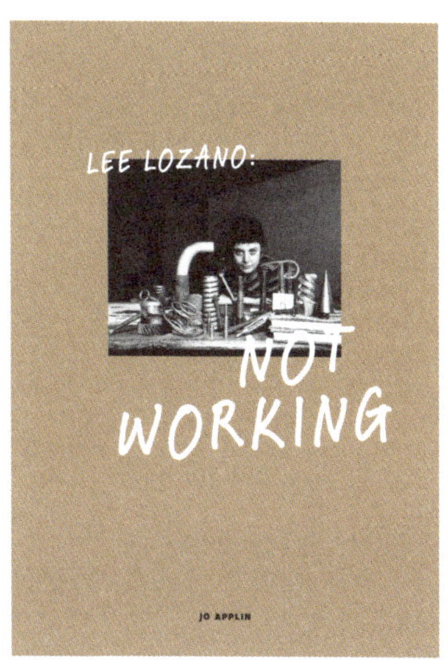

LEE LOZANO

LANGUAGE PIECES

Lee Lozano: Language Pieces
(Fruitmarket Gallery and Hauser
& Wirth Publishers, 2018) is the
definitive collection of Lozano's text-
based "language pieces." Originally
handwritten in her notebooks, Lozano
would often transcribe these works
onto large sheets of paper or type them.
These larger versions were intended
as artworks and are still exhibited
today. This book presents forty-six
of these works as full-scale facsimiles
and is a crucial document of Lozano's
pioneering conceptual practice.

Private Books 1–9 (Karma, 2016–21) is a collection of Lozano's private notebooks, which the artist kept between 1968 and 1970 while she was living in New York. In 1972 she returned to the books and rigorously edited them, sometimes crossing out entire pages. These notebooks unflinchingly document Lozano's daily life, relationships, and political and philosophical feelings about art and the art world around her. At the time of publication, nine of the eleven extant notebooks have been published as facsimiles.

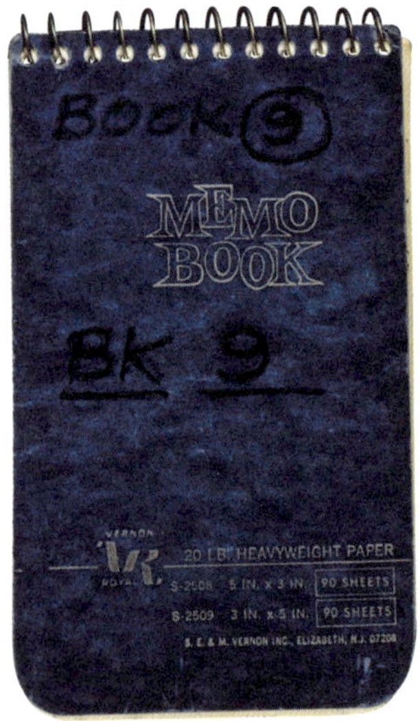

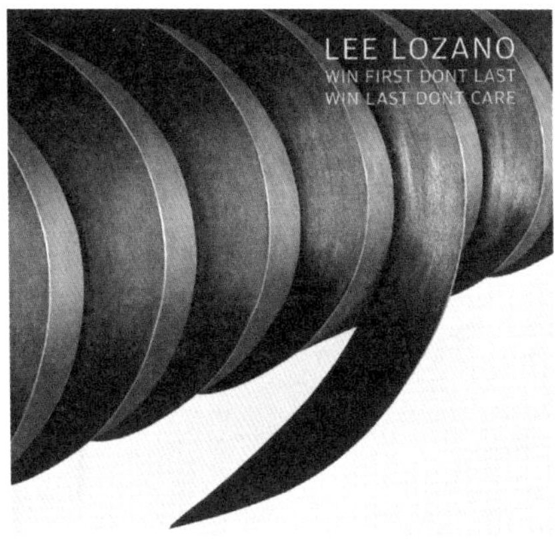

Lee Lozano: Win First Don't Last Win Last Don't Care (Kunsthalle Basel and the Van Abbemuseum, 2006) accompanied Lozano's exhibition at Kunsthalle Basel and the Van Abbemuseum, Eindhoven. Edited by Adam Szymczyk, this publication comprehensively documents Lozano's practice through photographs, writings, and a rich collection of archival material. Essays by Todd Alden and Helen Molesworth are accompanied by archival writings by Jill Johnston and Lozano.

Videos about Lozano's life and work can be accessed via the code above. They include a conversation between Melissa Rachleff, Barry Rosen and Jaap van Liere of the Estate of Lee Lozano, and Randy Kennedy, director of special projects at Hauser & Wirth, placing Lozano's early work in the downtown New York art world of the 1960s; a walkthrough of Lozano's 2020 exhibition at Hauser & Wirth Sommerset, led by art historian Jo Applin, offering an insightful discussion of Lozano's early paintings and works on paper; a talk by art historian Tamar Garb probing issues of gender, sexuality, and privacy in Lozano's work, held on the occasion of the exhibition *Lee Lozano: c. 1962* at Hauser & Wirth London; and a conversation between the curators of *Lee Lozano: Strike*, Lucrezia Calabrò Visconti and Sarah Cosulich, presenting a thoughtful introduction to the exhibition and the political defiance at the core of Lozano's oeuvre.

Sources

Most of the quotations from Lozano are from her notebooks. At the time of publication, nine of her eleven extant notebooks have been published as facsimiles by Karma (New York, 2016–21); her unpublished notebooks were provided by The Estate of Lee Lozano. Where a quotation appears as written text illustrated elsewhere in this book, the page number is provided below.

p. 15: "I can't 'hang' with work…" is from Lozano's February 8, 1969, entry in *Private Book 1* (New York: Karma, 2016), n.p. "Total personal and public revolution" is from Lozano's *General Strike Piece*, 1969; ill., p. 33.

pp. 16, 109: "The hardest work I have ever done" is from Lozano's April 5, 1970, entry in *Private Book 8* (New York: Karma, 2021), pp. 114–15; ill., p. 107.

p. 18: "Seek the extremes…" is from Lozano's *Grass Piece*, 1969; ill., p. 31.

p. 19: "Maybe the idea of 'destroy in order to create'…" is from Lozano's May 14, 1968, entry in *Private Book 1*, n.p.

p. 21: The chapter title "Everyone knows that an artist's best work…" is from a lecture Lozano delivered at the Nova Scotia College of Art and Design on July 16, 1971; an excerpt appears on pp. 112–13. The full lecture is reproduced in *Win First Don't Last Win Last Don't Care*, ed. Adam Szymczyk (Basel: Kunsthalle Basel; Eindhoven: Van Abbemuseum, 2006), pp. 162–70. "The Scorpio version of shift" is from Lozano's May 21, 1969, entry in *Private Book 2* (New York: Karma, 2017), p. 49.

p. 29: Lozano's response to Alan Saret appears in Lozano's June 22, 1969, entry in *Private Book 2*, p. 82. "The way a junkie looks at his arm" is from a May 1968 entry in *Private Book 1*, n.p.

pp. 29–30: "Lee was extraordinarily intense…" is from Lucy Lippard, "Lee Lozano," *Artforum* 40, no. 2 (October 2001): p. 129.

p. 30: "Not dictator to anybody…" is from Lozano's April 24, 1969, entry in *Private Book 2*, pp. 12–13.

pp. 40, 142: "Rejection of traditional American middle-class female trip" is from an untitled artwork from 1970.

pp. 40–41: "Lozano (the name) snapped off" is from an untitled artwork dated September 8, 1971; ill., p. 137. "Redesign yourself…" is from Lozano's *Infofiction Prologue Aug 17 68 Riff*, 1968.

p. 50: Lozano's response to Robert Morris's article appears in her April 17, 1968, entry in *Private Book 1*, n.p.

p. 61: "Great puns are metaphor in its purest form" is from an undated entry in *Private Book 1*, n.p. "Compucianism" is from an undated entry in *Private Book 8*, p. 71.

p. 66: "Become a gas, a charge, a force…" is from *Infofiction Prologue Aug 17 68 Riff*, 1968.

p. 67: The quotes "if I were an old-fashioned man…" and "science is on my mind all the time…" are from an undated entry in *Private Book 1*, n.p. "Everything 'important'…" is from Lozano's July 28, 1968, entry in *Private Book 1*, n.p.

p. 81: The quotes "whoever or whatever designed human beings…" and "let the eyes be redesigned to look inward as well as out" are from *Infofiction Prologue Aug 17 68 Riff*, 1968.

p. 91: "When you're 'trying to make it'…" is from an untitled piece dated February 1969 that appears in *Private Book 1*, n.p.

p. 94: "my art is about t.!…" is from an undated entry in *Private Book 9* (New York: Karma, 2021), p. 18. "I don't get spaced on dope…" is from an undated entry in *Private Book 9*, p. 15.

p. 96: "as a result of the multi-dimensionality…" is from Lozano's May 11, 1968, entry in *Private Book 1*, n.p.

p. 97: "Both grass & no-grass states produce fantasy…" is from Lozano's May 6, 1969, entry in *Private Book 1*, n.p.

p. 102 "Women have been tricked…" is from an undated entry in *Private Book 6* (New York: Karma, 2019), pp. 16–17.

pp. 102–3: The chapter title and quote "I am not a feminist" is from an undated entry in *Private Book 1*, n.p.

p. 107: "artpigs & artrats" in from an undated entry in *Private Book 1*, n.p.

p. 108: "Pass (piss? watch out!) on ideas…" is from an undated entry in *Private Book 2*, n.p. "NYC: a decade of competitiveness…" is from Lozano's May 2, 1970, entry in *Private Book 9*, p. 2.

p. 109: "It was inevitable, since I work in sets…" is from Lozano's April 5, 1970, entry in *Private Book 8*, pp. 114–17; ill., p. 107.

pp. 109–10: "Start living at more random hours…" is from an undated entry in *Private Book 7* (New York: Karma, 2019), p. 117.

p. 110: "Some institutions I do not believe in…" is a June 1968 entry from *Private Book 1*, n.p.; ill., p. 110.

p. 111: "Dropout only works along with diminished consumption…" is from an undated entry in *Private Book 8*, p. 120.

p. 114: "The dialogues are a saying goodbye?" is from Lozano's July 3, 1969, entry in *Private Book 2*, p. 88.

p. 122: "What if I stopped doing different pieces…" is from Lozano's May 19, 1969, entry in *Private Book 2*, p. 47.

p. 131: "Whitney Museum: How does it feel…" is from an undated entry in Lozano's "Private Book 11," 1970, p. 10; ill., p. 129. "the same jibberjabber allcunt disorder…" is from Lozano's *Women's Lib Brought Bad Luck*, 1970–71; ill., p. 133.

p. 135–36: "Just about right" and "she always hoped she would" are from an undated entry in *Private Book 2*, p. 54; ill, p. 134. The "'striking' structural similarity between…" is from an undated entry in *Private Book 2*, p. 7. "I have no identity…" and "I will renounce the artist's ego…" are from an untitled artwork dated September 8, 1971; ill., p. 137.

p. 138: The chapter title "All ends are loose ends because there are no hard edges in the universe" is from an undated entry in *Private Book 2*, p. 30.

p. 139: "Why do you need roots when you have gravity" is from Lozano's January 2, 1969, entry in *Private Book 5* (New York: Karma, 2018), p. 47.

Additional Captions

Cover: Lozano at the opening of *The New Art*, Davison Center, Wesleyan University, Middletown, Connecticut, 1964

pp. 4–11: Lozano lecturing at the Nova Scotia College of Art and Design, Halifax, July 16, 1971

p. 12: No title, 1963. Graphite and crayon on paper, 10¾ × 13¾ in. (27.4 × 35 cm)

p. 13: No title, 1963. Crayon on paper, 10¾ × 13¾ in. (27.4 × 35 cm)

p. 152: *Questionnaire*, 1998. Ink on paper, 11 × 8½ in. (27.9 × 21.6 cm)

Credits

E

QUESTIONNAIRE, WITH JOKES,
CONCERNING PURCHASES & PURCHASERS
OF MY ART.

NUMBER OF PURCHASES.

INFO ABOUT PURCHASERS. INDICATE AGE GROUPS.

    PURCHASERS WHO WERE INDIVIDUALS, NUMBER OF.

        HETER COUPLES, " "

        GROUPS, " "

        U.S., " "

        EUROPEAN, " "

        ASIAN, OR OTHER, " "

        COLLEGE EDUCATED, PERCENTAGE OF.

    CLASS OF PURCHASERS, BETTER, " "

        MIDDLE, " "

        WORKING, " "

RELIGIONS OF PURCHASERS, IN PERCENTAGES.

OCCUPATIONS OF PURCHASERS, NUMBER OF.

    BUSINESS MEN.

    PROFESSIONAL MEN.

    ACADEMIC MEN.

    POLITICIANS.

    MEN WHO WERE ARTISTS, OR IN THE ARTS.

    SCIENTISTS.

    PUBLISHERS.

    RICH.

GENDER OF PURCHASERS, PERCENTAGE OF

    MALE HOMOSEXUALS.

PURPOSE OF PURCHASES, NUMBER OF, FOR

    HOME,

    MUSEUM.

    OFFICE.

    SCHOOL.

    SPECULATION.

    RESALE, GALLERY,

    COLLECTIONS,

OTHER RELEVANT INFO,

FOR BARRY & YAAP, NY   INVENTED IN AUG, SEPT & OCT, WRITTEN

In the Studio: Lee Lozano
© 2025 Hauser & Wirth Publishers

All texts © 2025 the authors
Additional copyright credits on p. 151

ISBN: 978-3-907493-19-9
ISSN: 3042-5751
Library of Congress Control Number:
2025940305

Available through ARTBOOK | D.A.P.
(North and South America) and
Thames & Hudson (all other territories)

Series design: Fraser Muggeridge studio
Printed in Italy

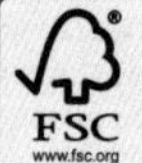